D0060615

"In *Evolutionary Enlightenment,* Andrew Cohen has given us a compellingly new, important, even profound work on the nature of spiritual enlightenment in today's world. Enlightenment is still viewed as a nondual realization—a 'not-twoness' of Absolute and relative, Emptiness and Form. But in our time, the relative domain of Form has discovered itself to be evolving, and a truly non-dual realization is thus a not-twoness of Timeless Being and Evolving Becoming. More than an intellectual discussion, this is a book of practice, of actually how to realize this new Evolutionary Enlightenment. It is truly one of the most significant books on spirituality written in the postmodern world."

**—Ken Wilber,** author of *The Integral Vision*

"Andrew Cohen maps out a path to be the change we not only should *want* to see in the world but that we objectively and urgently *need* in the world. Whether we take his path or look to another, we should read what he has to say, for it is based on deep personal experience that has proven meaningful for thousands and thousands."

**—Ervin Laszlo,** author of *Science and the Reenchantment of the Cosmos*

"Like Sri Aurobindo, the great spiritual and evolutionary pathfinder for the twentieth century, in Andrew Cohen we have just such a pathfinder for our own era. In Andrew's writing, as in his person, we experience directly the living Eros of the divine, urging always toward transformation and ultimately toward evolution."

**—Allan Combs, PhD,** author of *Consciousness Explained Better*

"Cohen not only describes the territory of Evolutionary Enlightenment, he provides the vehicle for making the journey. In a wise and generous voice he describes how—not in some future time but now—each of us can respond to the evolutionary impulse seeking to emerge in, through, and as every human being, birthing an enlightened society."

**—Michael Bernard Beckwith,** author of *Spiritual Liberation*

"This is not your standard spiritual book. It is not your standard book on achieving the bliss of enlightenment. We are far more than we think we are, says Andrew Cohen. We are the cosmos come alive. We are 'the evolutionary impulse' incarnate. We are the cosmos's way of becoming something new, of turning that which does not yet exist into a reality. Andrew Cohen's Evolutionary Enlightenment isn't easy. But, argues Cohen, it is worth it."

—**Howard Bloom,** author of *The Lucifer Principle*

"We are living in a time of profound transformation. Learning to navigate the dynamic changes that are unfolding offers each of us the chance to embrace our role as conscious agents in the evolutionary process. Cohen's insightful book takes us into this dynamic process, empowering us to co-create a future for our collective awakening."

—**Marilyn Schlitz, PhD,** President and CEO, Institute of Noetic Sciences

"Andrew Cohen's *Evolutionary Enlightenment* adds to the vision of evolutionary panentheism that is emerging in the world today. His simultaneous embrace of our ever-present (though ordinarily hidden) oneness with God and our ever-developing life here on Earth, I believe, embodies the philosophic stance we need to take to fulfill our deepest calling and best serve the world at large."

—**Michael Murphy,** author of *The Future of the Body*

"Andrew Cohen is the most precise teacher of the essence of spiritual conscious evolution and its social contribution. He has identified the impulse of evolution as our own subjective yearning to create, and he has given us ways of cultivating that creativity as a spiritual path toward authentic selfhood. This is the growing edge of spiritual/social evolution and he is on it."

—**Barbara Marx Hubbard,** author of *Conscious Evolution*

"If the fourteen-billion-year cosmic experiment that resulted in our lives is not to end in the next few centuries, it will require brave and brilliant steps in our spiritual evolution. With instruction at once tough and tender, Andrew Cohen gives us the inspiration and the means to accomplish the greatest of all endeavors for the human spirit. This is a spiritual masterpiece."

—**Jean Houston, PhD,** author of *A Mythic Life*

"Andrew Cohen is a truly remarkable spiritual teacher on the cutting edge of evolutionary thinking and action. He and his students are playing an invaluable leadership role in the emergence of evolutionary spirituality: an integrity-based, deeply meaningful approach to life grounded in our best scientific understandings of cosmic, earth, biological, and human history. Andrew's writings and teachings are destined to make a real difference in the world."

—**Michael Dowd,** author of *Thank God for Evolution*

"Andrew Cohen has given us a clear, practical, and empowering guidebook on how to cross the historic threshold that leads from the unsustainable world we see already crumbling around us today toward a vibrant future reflective of our best human selves. Instead of wishfully waiting for it to happen, he shows us how we can, responsibly and immediately, begin co-creating this future now. To do so requires what Andrew describes as 'spiritual courage,' mastery of his Tenets of Evolutionary Enlightenment, and forging the profoundly new, transformational culture he envisions—which we might call a culture of possibility."

—**Gordon Dveirin, EdD,** and **Joan Borysenko, PhD,** authors of *Your Soul's Compass*

"There is a place for stillness and there is a time for action. The twenty-first century is the period in history when those who feel the call must boldly take a stand. Read Andrew Cohen's book, and gain a fresh insight into the nature of enlightenment itself and how you can help make a better tomorrow through your own evolutionary involvement."

—**Roshi Vernon Kitabu Turner,** author of *Soul to Soul*

"Andrew Cohen has arrived at an insight that is crucial for our historical situation. Enlightenment is not a movement out of the everyday world but is instead a profound entrance into deep participation in the evolution of the universe. Rarely have I encountered such simple, searing wisdom connecting religious ideas about enlightenment with the scientific understanding of an evolutionary cosmos."

—**Brian Swimme, PhD,** author of *The Universe Story*

"In *Evolutionary Enlightenment*, Andrew Cohen urges his readers to contribute to the crucial yet arduous process in which the Divine actualizes itself in history. While valorizing the traditional spiritual path that leads toward eternal divine Being, Cohen maintains that today's seeker has the opportunity and perhaps even the obligation to undertake the demanding transformation needed to contribute to the next phase in cosmic evolution. In his beautifully written book, well informed by major trends in developmental thinking, Cohen makes a substantial contribution to contemporary discussions about appropriate spiritual goals."

**—Michael E. Zimmerman,** Professor of Philosophy, University of Colorado

"Andrew Cohen's passionate engagement with tensions at the heart of creativity give strength to his call for an individual and collective evolutionary leap forward. He invites us to step beyond being to becoming, to face our own bewilderment and invent a culture of higher consciousness."

**—Alex Grey,** visionary artist and author of *Transfigurations*

"If you think that Andrew Cohen's latest book will be yet another description of traditional 'enlightenment' then you will be in for a huge surprise. It all starts with the big bang and appears to be endless as God emerges through each of us. I was thrilled with what I was reading for it resonated so powerfully with the 'levels of being' in the Clare W. Graves conceptual pattern. *Evolutionary Enlightenment* is a well-written companion piece to what we understand as the developmental spiral within people and cultures. I recommend it without reservation."

**—Don Edward Beck, PhD,** author of *Spiral Dynamics*
and founder of Centers for Human Emergence

# Evolutionary Enlightenment

# Evolutionary Enlightenment

## A New Path to Spiritual Awakening

ANDREW COHEN

SelectBooks, Inc.
*New York*

This edition published by SelectBooks, Inc.
For information address SelectBooks, Inc., New York, New York.

First Edition

ISBN 978-1-59079-209-4


*Cataloging-in-Publication Data*

Cohen, Andrew, 1955 Oct. 23-
  Evolutionary enlightenment : a new path to spiritual awakening / Andrew Cohen.
      p. cm.
  Summary: "The author presents a contemporary approach to the traditional ideal of personal enlightenment. Reinterpreting spiritual enlightenment as a means to evolve consciousness and culture in the context of a cosmic evolution, Cohen discusses the dimensions of the self, the role of meditation, and his Five Fundamental Tenets of Evolutionary Enlightenment"--Provided by publisher.
  Includes index.
  ISBN 978-1-59079-209-4 (hardbound : alk. paper)
  1. Spiritual life. I. Title.
  BL624.C612 2011
  204'.4--dc22
                                                    2011006198


Manufactured in the United States of America
10  9  8  7  6  5  4  3  2

*To Ken Wilber*
*for his Big Mind and Big Heart*

# CONTENTS

Contents

# FOREWORD
# by Deepak Chopra

WHEN BOOKS SPEAK TO YOU PERSONALLY, you hear the author's voice whispering, not just in your ear but to your deepest yearning. Andrew Cohen did that for me, making me believe something I long to be true: *There has never been a better time to be enlightened.*

When I was a child, it was easy to feel left behind. I was born too late to shoot arrows beside Arjuna, meditate under the Bodhi tree with the Buddha, or sit on an olive-covered hillside in Galilee hearing the Sermon on the Mount. There is a pervasive sense, even in advanced spiritual circles, that we are looking over our shoulders at the epochs when humans were closer to God or to their souls or to the promise of *Moksha.*

So it's heartening to hear a teacher who insists, with passion and a clear voice, that we haven't been left behind. This is only one of the messages to be found in these pages. Andrew has the pulse of modern life at his fingertips. His diagnosis of the demands and distractions of our noisy, busy world shows the accuracy of a skilled diagnostician. But long ago, when I spent many hours a day diagnosing patients, I learned that none of them would take any advice until they understood, quite basically, what the first step to healing needed to be. That first step was always the same: "You're going to get better." Reassurance is medicine, even if it can't be bottled, and in this book Andrew touched me with a deep sense of reassurance: *Don't worry. There's a place for the seeker. The universe has collaborated to bring you here, to this moment, so that you can wake up.*

The famous adage is wrong: The journey of a thousand miles doesn't begin with the first step. It begins with the assurance that you can take the first step. Many people lack that assurance, for all kinds of reasons. Some feel unworthy to seek beyond the limited territory of the known; some feel trapped behind walls or inwardly blocked; some feel paralyzed by timidity, fear, doubt, and skepticism in all their dubious coloring. When Andrew asks, *Why do some people develop a passion for spirituality while others don't?*, the answer he gives agrees perfectly with my own perspective: they haven't awakened to the evolutionary impulse within.

There's another famous adage that *is* true, about the spark that is enough to burn down a whole forest. Speaking literally, it means that a glimpse of your authentic self—which Andrew identifies with the impulse to evolve—will be so appealing that you cannot help but follow where your own growth leads. We know that this is a natural tendency. Children are eager to pass through every stage of development. Being five years old holds no allure when over the next horizon you can be six and then seven and eight. This automatic process has a magic hidden inside it that few realize. As a child develops, he (or she) doesn't have to lose who he is today in order to become who he will be tomorrow. Children happily remain who they are, while at a deeper level the future is unfolding the next stage of their growth.

We lose touch with that magic once we grow up and, as Wordsworth said, "the world is too much with us; late and soon." I know of no one else who is so intent on reinstating that magic as Andrew Cohen, and the means is simple: reconnect with the evolutionary impulse. That impulse began beyond space and time, in the domain of pure consciousness. It manifested in physical form and thus became shrouded by the mask of materialism. The human mind became distracted by the dance of *maya*. For all these reasons, the evolutionary impulse needed to be revealed again and described in detail, as this book does so beautifully. And I second Andrew's point that traditional spirituality focused too much on escapism, other worlds, withdrawal, and fatalism about the conduct of affairs in a corrupt world.

By definition, the evolutionary impulse changes its focus as human society shifts. In the sixth century BCE, the average person lived on the brink of survival. His needs and worries were drastic, and therefore it was seductive to retreat into a private world of peace and silence. Once there, communion with the transcendent proved immensely fascinating. But it was also true that to limit spirit to inner peace—or even the inner world—was misleading. Transcendence permeates everything; there is only one reality, deriving from the same source.

The problem is that each of us lives in duality, and our minds have been shaped to look upon duality as real. We have divided selves, and we perceive the world in terms of opposites, like right and wrong, good and evil, light and darkness. How can we transform ourselves to reach unity when duality is the only vehicle we have? A fish would have an easier time trying to get dry. After brilliantly unraveling the nature of duality and how it has captivated us, this book prescribes a cure for the divided self. I was particularly attracted to the five chapter headings that describe the Tenets of Evolutionary Enlightenment:

- Clarity of Intention
- The Power of Volition
- Face Everything and Avoid Nothing
- The Process Perspective
- Cosmic Conscience

Here, I think, Andrew reveals the core of self-transformation, and since each key is so critical, I'd like to comment on them in turn.

*Clarity of Intention*: Nothing is more powerful than intention, because it brings together three ingredients: desire, steadiness of purpose, and depth of awareness. These are the three facets of *Samyama*, as it is known in the Indian tradition. When a person has mastered *Samyama*, his every intent has the entire cosmos behind it or, to sound less grand, what you want is what the evolutionary impulse wants to give you.

Clarity, then, is more than saying, "I really, really know I want to be rich"—or any other dream that we'd like to have fulfilled. Instead, clarity means that you have used self-awareness to acquire the three aspects of *Samyama*:

You have a desire that is in keeping with your overall evolution and growth.

Your purpose is steady enough that you can follow the universe's response to your desire, wherever it leads.

You are established deep enough in your awareness that the right messages can come through and be heard—after all, you cannot receive or act upon what you aren't aware of. I've only described the basics, as they have impressed me personally. Andrew goes into more detail and gives an immensely valuable transpersonal, enlightened perspective.

*The Power of Volition*: Here Andrew touches on an ancient teaching, *Aham Brahmasmi*, or "I am the universe." This principle is close to my heart, because I find it unthinkable to be enlightened in a world of darkness and ignorance. Tradition holds otherwise, at least the reclusive tradition that impelled spiritual seekers to leave the world behind or retreat in solitude. In India, one hears various swamis and yogis calling the world "the mud" in contrast to their own spiritual place of purity, usually in the high, clear air of the Himalayas.

You can't treat sick patients and try to alleviate pain while still considering them as creatures of "the mud." I am of the mud, too, and so is everyone. It is our responsibility to change the environment on all levels, beginning with the spiritual, if human beings are to make the next evolutionary leap. Andrew's call to responsibility is as clarion and bracing as any I have ever heard.

*Face Everything and Avoid Nothing*: Andrew calls this principle, quite rightly I think, the "liberation of awareness." We are all imprisoned by the limits of what we call normal awareness, and the evolutionary impulse wants, above all else, to make us free. William Blake said much the same thing about "mind-forged manacles," and thus Andrew joins a long line of inspired visionaries. What he has added to this lineage is once again reassuring. If you face everything in life, you won't be left exposed and vulnerable, like a sea creature wrenched from its shell and left quivering in the blazing sun. That is only our fear, which is why we keep delaying the confrontations that take more existential courage than we think we possess.

Instead, we need to be reassured that facing everything is in keeping with our own evolution. Nothing is more natural than to evolve; it entails neither struggle nor fear. Andrew's path still requires courage. Breakthroughs cannot help but have the word "break" in them, and dismantling our old conditioning does confront us with feelings and memories it would be far easier to bury. What makes such ruptures bearable—indeed, most desirable—is that in facing everything, we awaken dormant powers inside that can cope with anything. A prisoner can fashion a kind of comfortable world within a small, confined space, but that is nothing compared to the power of liberation.

*The Process Perspective*: When you are willing to look at everything about your life, it ceases to be "your" life. That is, it belongs not to an isolated individual who can be labeled according to convenient tags:

your likes and dislikes, your race and religion, who you love and who is your enemy. An impersonal view emerges instead. "Impersonal" isn't a word to make the heart beat with hope, but I think Andrew is right to use it. An easier synonym might be "universal." The small self evolves into the universal self. You discover your true status as a child of the cosmos.

Keeping your cosmic birthright in mind isn't easy when somebody rear-ends you in traffic or the person you are infatuated with isn't infatuated with you. Better to focus on process, taking each step as it comes, fitting the small stones littering the shore into a grand mosaic. Andrew's emphasis on process is for me one of the most valuable practical aspects of following the evolutionary impulse.

*Cosmic Conscience*: Many readers will blink twice at this phrase, hoping that it says cosmic consciousness—but Andrew means *conscience*. We all know why the other wording is seductive. Enlightenment is like one big paycheck, and having worked for it year after year, we expect to be showered with spiritual riches—or richness—that the rest of the world will admire. It's a comforting fantasy on those long dark nights of the soul, or shadowy afternoons. But the evolutionary impulse looks after the future of *all*; therefore, its conscience, if we may use that term, is vigilant about what is good for everyone, leaving out no living creature.

It is wise and right for Andrew to call us to have such a conscience. It doesn't miraculously descend on you on the day when you are noticed to be a saint rather than a normal person. Cosmic conscience is part of the passion for evolution, so the more you yearn to be transformed, the more you see yourself intertwined with all living things. This viewpoint stands out in high relief in the Buddha's teachings, but Andrew has couched it in modern terms, as he has the rest of this eye-opening, unique book.

The five tenets of enlightened living are enough to change the world. How many times have you heard that said, while thinking to yourself, "but nothing will really change. The world will go on the way it has always gone on." In this case, the opposite is true. The world cannot help but change; the cosmic plan has been evolutionary since the beginning, and before. No one can escape the process of evolution. We can blind ourselves to it; we can join the side of the resistance to change. Conscious choice makes a difference. But when asked what would happen if a person didn't wake up to the evolutionary impulse, a wise teacher once replied, "The divine plan doesn't need you in order to succeed. But you can choose to have it succeed through you." Which is the choice the following pages present, with great imagination and insight.

## ACKNOWLEDGMENTS

FIRST AND FOREMOST, I want to thank and bow deeply to all of my teachers, most especially H.W.L. Poonja, who set me free. I want to thank all of my students, past and present, whose dedication and commitment to my vision has enabled me to give rise to emergent potentials I could never have brought forth on my own. I also want to extend my gratitude for the profound influence of contemporary evolutionary and integral pioneers, especially Brian Swimme, Don Beck, and Ken Wilber, along with many others, who have helped enormously to deepen and refine my thinking and understanding. I want to thank Deepak Chopra for writing such a heartfelt foreword to this book. I would like to thank Arielle Ford for extending herself so generously to support this project from its inception. I would also like to thank my agent Bill Gladstone for believing so passionately in the power and significance of this teaching for our time, and Kenzi Sugihara and the team at SelectBooks for being so gracious and easy to work with. Finally, I want to express my deep appreciation to my student, editor, colleague, and friend Ellen Daly for the years we have spent in creative collaboration on the articulation of my teachings, and for the countless hours she spent bringing my spoken word into a form that we could then together shape into this book.

*Andrew Cohen*
*Lenox, Massachusetts*
*April 2011*

**PART I**

# A Cosmic Journey

# A Longing to Evolve

WHY DO SOME OF US seek higher truths? Why is it that certain individuals are driven blindly, madly, and passionately to transcend their own limitations? Why do we, at times, feel compelled to improve ourselves, not only for our own sake but for the sake of a higher cause that we can sense yet barely see? Why is it that in those precious moments when we are most conscious and most awake, we seem to intuit a deeper sense of purpose that is infinitely bigger than our personal worlds can contain? What is that soft vibration that tugs at our hearts and beckons us to courageously leap beyond the small confines of the separate self so that we can participate in the life-process in a much deeper and more authentic way?

That vibration is none other than the spiritual impulse, the impulse to evolve at the level of consciousness. It could be that same impulse that caused you to pick up this book and, no doubt, that compelled me to write it. And it's not just a feeling that you or I might have. This impulse is something much bigger. In fact, I believe it is that very same impulse that caused something to come from nothing fourteen billion years ago, that compelled an entire material universe to miraculously emerge from complete emptiness. To me, at least, there is no doubt that a great and mysterious energy and intelligence with enormous power is driving this entire evolutionary process forward in every moment. And our own direct personal experience of spiritual inspiration is the most tangible expression of that very same drive.

Since that inspiration first awoke in me, more than three decades ago, it has taken me on an extraordinary journey. And during this time, I have discovered something very important that few people seem to know: *This spiritual impulse moves in two directions simultaneously.* If we follow one direction, it will carry us far into the distant future, and if we follow the other, it will take us back to before the beginning of time. The path that most mystics in the enlightenment tradition have taken is not the future-oriented one; it is the perennial meditative path that countless seekers have followed for millennia in pursuit of spiritual illumination. And this traditional approach is not future-oriented—it is not time-oriented at all. Traditional enlightenment points us beyond the world, beyond time and space, toward what has been the perennial source, at least until now, of spiritual freedom and mystical liberation: the ground of Being. But I believe that those of us in the twenty-first century at the leading edge of consciousness and culture urgently need a mystical spirituality and a source of soul liberation that points us not beyond time but toward the future that we need to create. I believe the spiritual impulse today is calling us not away from the world but toward that big next step we need to take *in* our world. That next step will not emerge by itself—it must be consciously created by human beings who have awakened to the same impulse that is driving the process. Awakening to that energy and intelligence is what this book is all about, because that is the source of the new enlightenment.

There's so much I want to tell you about this new enlightenment, but before I do, I need to tell you a little bit about the traditional one. It is, after all, the foundation for everything I'm about to describe. Its territory is subtle and profound and can be easily misunderstood. But it's worth making the effort to try to truly understand enlightenment, because within its mysteries we can find some of the most important and liberating truths that human beings have ever discovered. That's why the opening chapters are dedicated wholeheartedly to transmitting the experience of traditional enlightenment. They aspire to convey, through the written word, the actual state of consciousness and liberating perspective that emerges when we follow the spiritual impulse all the way back to before the beginning of time, and transcend the mind, ego, and world in a dramatic way. But once we have arrived there, and tasted the primordial freedom that has been the goal of mystics throughout the ages, like many people at our unique time in history, we will find ourselves compelled not to rest there, but to reenter the fray of the creative process. And this spiritual rebirth, as the evolutionary impulse embodied in human form, is what the majority of this book, and the teaching of Evolutionary Enlightenment, is all about.

# CHAPTER 1

# Back to Before the Beginning

IN ORDER TO FIND OUT FOR YOURSELF what the timeless ideal of enlightenment is all about, the first step you need to take is a very big one. You have to be willing, at least temporarily, to let absolutely everything go. You have to take an inner journey beyond everything you are and everything you know, beyond time, form, thought, and memory, all the way back to before the beginning, before anything ever happened, before the universe was born.

Before the beginning, there was no time, no form, and no space—only absolute emptiness. Before the beginning, there was nothing ... but you were there.

You don't have to take my word for this—you can discover the truth of it in your very own experience right now, if you are willing to take that radical step and let go—let go of thought and feeling, time and world, self and other. You can discover the timeless, eternal answer to the question "Who am I?"—the answer that liberates you from any and all sense of limitation. The journey you will take, beyond time and form, is the very same that the greatest realizers have taken, and the answer you will find is the very same that set them free. You will discover the source of enlightenment itself.

In order to answer the question "Who am I?", in order to go back to before the beginning within your own experience, you have to put your attention on the deepest sense of what it feels like to be yourself right now, and simultaneously let everything else go. Letting go means falling so deeply into yourself that all that is left is empty space.

To discover that infinite depth in your own self, you must find a way to enter into a deep state of meditation—so deep that your awareness of thought moves into the background and eventually disappears. As your awareness detaches itself from the thought-stream, your identification with emotion and memory begins to fall away. When awareness of thought disappears, awareness of the passing of time disappears along with it. If you keep penetrating into the infinite depths of your own self, even your awareness of your own physical form will disappear.

If you go deep enough, letting your attention expand and release from all objects in consciousness, you will find that all the structures of the created universe begin to crumble before your eyes. Awareness itself—limitless, empty, pristine—becomes the only object of your attention.

As your attention is released from the conditioned mind-process, freed from the confines of the body and the boundaries of the personal self-sense, the inner dimension of your own experience begins to open up to an immeasurable degree. Imagine that you have been fast asleep in a small, dark chamber, then suddenly awaken to find yourself floating in the infinite expanse of a vast, peaceful ocean. That's what this journey to the depths of your own self feels like. You become aware of a limitless dimension that you did not even know was there. Moments before, you may have experienced yourself as being trapped, a prisoner of your body, mind, and emotions. But when you awaken to this new dimension, all sense of confinement disappears. You find yourself resting in, and as, boundless empty space.

In that empty space, the mind is completely still; there is no time, no memory, not even a trace of personal history. And the deeper you fall into that space, the more everything will continue to fall away, until finally all that will be left is you. When you let absolutely everything go—body, mind, memory, and time—you will find, miraculously, that you still exist. In fact, in the end, you discover that all that exists is you!

WHY IS THIS EXPERIENCE SIGNIFICANT? Because the infinite space you awaken to is not only a quiet place inside your own head—it's a deeper dimension of reality itself.

Reality *as a whole*—the seen and the unseen, the known and the unknown, all that ever was and ever could be—is made up of two dimensions. We could call these the manifest and the unmanifest. Most of the time, we are only aware of the manifest dimension, the domain of time and space and becoming. But like an iceberg floating in the ocean, only visible above the surface but extending far below, the reality we see is resting on an unseen, unknown, unfathomable dimension. We cannot see or touch or grasp this dimension because it is, by its very nature, unmanifest. But you can experientially discover that unmanifest domain when you let go of thought, feeling, time, and world—that static and unchanging, beginningless and endless, timeless and formless dimension that is the foundation of all that is.

You cannot go any deeper into yourself than the unmanifest dimension. *There is nowhere else to go.* Everything begins and that primordial emptiness, which is why the mystics call it th of Being. As you cease to identify with objects, that timeless, spaceless, infinite no-place emerges as the very nature of your own unborn self. All sense of boundary, any sense of limitation, including all memory and desire, dissolves in an effulgent sea of completeness that always *already* exists.

When you sink below the surface of the manifest world and awaken to the timeless depth of that empty ground, you find yourself contemplating consciousness in its primordial state, free from all content, before it entered the stream of time. In this dimension, nothing has ever happened. The universe has not yet emerged; you have not been born; even time itself has not yet begun.

SCIENTISTS TELL US THAT WHEN TIME BEGAN, fourteen billion years ago, something came from nothing. When you awaken to the ground of Being, you realize that when something came from nothing, the nothing didn't disappear. That unmanifest, unborn dimension is the ever-present ground out of which everything is still arising in every moment. It is what the Buddha called "the deathless," and what others call "eternity consciousness." When you awaken to this dimension in your own awareness, you will find yourself always already resting in the eternal moment before time began. This is the recognition that liberates: *Prior to everything, I already am.*

The experience of this recognition is not one of *becoming* liberated. It is of being *already* liberated. What you realize when you awaken to that ground is that there is a part of each and every one of us that is already free—from *everything*. That part of yourself, which is the ground of Being, has never been bound, trapped, or limited in any way. That's the part of yourself that I want you to discover. It's not the part of yourself that needs to *become* free. It is *already* free, right now.

THE GROUND OF BEING IS EMPTY. It is an objectless, timeless, spaceless, thoughtless void. And yet, there is something miraculously and mysteriously compelling about this empty no-place. When you take the journey I've been describing, you will discover this for yourself—beyond time, beyond thought, beyond self, beyond other, beyond world. When all these objects fall away, what is left is that ground. The ground of Being is not an object, and that is why it is sometimes described as zero. When you focus your attention upon zero, or no-thing whatsoever, you realize that it is immeasurable, unquantifiable, and ever-ungraspable by your linear, rational mind. The mind is accustomed to focusing on objects—that's what its function is. So when you try to focus on something that is not an object, the mind doesn't know what to do. But if *you* make a decision to contemplate zero, you can begin to penetrate beyond the dualistic perspective that defines most of your experience. When you focus upon zero—when something meditates upon nothing—a flip can occur that throws you beyond the mind and beyond time. What opens up is a nonconceptual dimension of perception that is not ordinarily apparent. Through the contemplation of zero, you drill a hole in the structures of your own ignorance and penetrate the mystery of consciousness.

The contemplation of consciousness—which is the contemplation of no-thing whatsoever—is endlessly fascinating. It's like staring at a candle in a dark night—you find yourself mesmerized by something that is unchanging yet infinitely compelling. You feel drawn into something you don't understand rationally but that your heart or soul grasps completely. You are drawn into it, and as you are drawn into it, the only thing you experience as real is the eternal or timeless nature of Being itself. You find yourself in a state of rapture, because the deepest part of yourself has been released from your ego's endless fears and concerns, and drawn out of the time process altogether.

The empty groundless ground of Being needs no external affirmation; it is always already perfect, fulfilled, and complete. But *it wants to know itself.* It is perpetually self-seeking, and when it finds itself, it is affirmed in its own self-discovery. All *Being* wants to do is delight in itself, forever, endlessly absorbed with its own infinite nature. It seems that the very essence of consciousness at the deepest level is this self-delight.

If you give attention to the empty ground of your own experience of consciousness, you will see that self-delight is its nature. Once again, consciousness is not an object. Consciousness is the *subject.* And the subject is perpetually meditating upon itself. Once you have located that pure subjectivity, and cultivated enough concentration to become aware of its qualities, you will discover that indeed there is something mysterious and infinitely compelling about the deepest level of consciousness. That is its absolute nature. Whether it has been five minutes or five years, when you rediscover that groundless ground, miraculously you will find that it is ever new.

This is why, when you awaken to that consciousness, you may feel as if "I could stay here forever." There is no impetus, no *desire* to do anything. And yet there is more to it than that. If there was simply no desire, that would be the *absence* of a certain quality. But consciousness has an undeniable *presence*. How can we describe this paradoxical quality of consciousness? Because consciousness is not an object, you cannot say it is some*thing*. And yet it is not nothing. Nothing is void; it has no attributes, no qualities. Consciousness is empty of any *thing*, and yet there is something endlessly captivating about that emptiness. As you contemplate its unmoving depths, you become aware of a presence that is so vast that its nature seems to be *everything*—fullness, completeness, perfection. The emptiness is full. That's why the emptiness is compelling, because it is full of the knowing of this mysterious everything that is not a thing. It's everything; it's nothing—you can go on forever: *everything ... nothing ... nothing ... everything,* always meaning the same thing. If you could say everything and nothing in one breath, perhaps that would capture the paradoxical nature of consciousness.

So the desirelessness of consciousness is connected to this paradoxical emptiness and fullness, to this overwhelming *presence* that is everything and nothing at once. This presence is so profound that we could use the word God as a metaphor for its absolute nature: already full, already complete, already perfect.

When you meditate upon the depths of consciousness, and become compelled by its utter desirelessness, its fullness and indescribable peace, you can have the experience of being aware of or in touch with God. When you directly experience the absolute peace of the unmanifest ground, you have no desire for the things of this world. Knowing that ground, you want nothing except *to be*: to have nothing, to know nothing, to be no one, for eternity. Beyond time, two hours or two hundred thousand years makes no difference. You are awake—awake and at peace, dwelling on the mystery of pure unmanifest Being. In blissful, ecstatic indifference, you wouldn't mind if the whole universe disappeared.

This is why you feel the sense that "I could stay here forever." When you find yourself feeling that way, you will understand why men and women throughout history have spent years, even lifetimes, meditating in caves. When you directly experience the ground of your own Being, you will understand that mysterious longing to be alone with God, forever.

# CHAPTER 2

# Nonduality

*Before everything that was and before everything that is, I already am.* This revelation is the ground of everything—the groundless ground of reality itself and the foundation of both traditional enlightenment and the new evolutionary enlightenment.

Mystical insight into this mystery of mysteries often occurs as a result of a deep and sincere practice of meditation, but it can also spontaneously erupt within an unsuspecting soul. When the mind or the filter of your cognitive apparatus quiets down, or temporarily becomes transparent, the whisper of intuition can reveal to you the liberating presence of that empty, infinite ground that exists beyond time. The immediacy of enlightened awareness emerges the moment you let go of the time process and all that it represents to the mind, ego, and personality. When there is no time you are free, right now. Pay attention to your own experience when you take that journey back to before the beginning: In the depths of your own self, is there any awareness of the passing of time? If you go deep enough, to that place where you feel that you could remain forever, you will recognize time to be the ultimate mirage. And it will become apparent to you that your attachment to time has been preventing you from discovering your own inherent freedom. No-time has no past and no future—only the liberating immediacy of the eternal present, which has no beginning and no end.

When you awaken in a dramatic way, you see the entire world of form and time, the whole universe, including your own personal history, from the perspective of that deepest part of yourself that *already IS*—the part of you that never entered into the stream of time in the first place.

*I have never been born, you realize, and therefore I can never die. The entire world, indeed the entire universe, is happening out there and I am always free from it. The Self alone is real because that is the only part of me that never changes.*

From this place of unconditional freedom and glorious detachment, you witness the entire unfolding of the creative process, and it all becomes transparent. Dare to let yourself see through the illusion of time. Dare to embrace that perspective that allows you to see that everything is part of a transitory, and therefore illusory, progression of birth and death. If you want to discover enlightenment, you need to go so deep that it becomes apparent to you, at least in that moment, that the Self alone is real. All else is a temporary illusion. *Trust in this alone and be free,* the sages tell us. *Remain detached and disengaged from all except that which is real, and you will be enlightened in this very life. The mind is an illusion. Time is an illusion. The world is an illusion. Only the Self is real.*

This is the peace you see in the eyes of the mystic, the smile on the face of the Buddha. It is the liberating knowledge that in that deepest part of your own self, *none of this ever happened.* When this becomes obvious to you, you will laugh that unmistakable laugh of one who knows the secret of secrets.

IT IS LITERALLY ENLIGHTENING TO FIND that when thought, time, world, and even your own body disappears, you haven't gone anywhere! That's the miracle of miracles and the mystery of mysteries. How is it that when everything disappears, including mind and memory, the most intimately felt essence of your own self remains? And how is it possible that the self that remains when time and form disappear is eternal and unchanging? That self has never been born and will never die.

From the perspective of the rational mind, a human life is a linear, limited event, circumscribed by the inescapable march of time from birth to death. But when you penetrate beyond the mind, you directly see, know, and feel that instead of merely being an individual body, mind, and personality that was born and is going to die, you are that empty ground of Being that has never become anything.

That primordial ground is who you *always* are, no matter how things may appear at any given moment in time; it is the very essence of your own self at its most fundamental level. How can you know that? Because, as we have discovered, when every attribute that you habitually identify as being *you* falls away, your deepest sense of self is still there. But that self has no name, no history, no gender, no personal identity. It is not really *your* self—it is *the* Self, the absolute subject. It is singular. Consciousness in this primordial state is the "I" of the entire cosmos—the subjectivity or interiority of everything that exists.

Consciousness has no boundaries, no beginning and no end. The cognitive faculties of the human mind cannot grasp its infinite nature, because we habitually relate to our own self as a fixed, finite entity, and to every object that we give our attention to as being fixed and finite also. Pay attention, and you will see that you are constantly locating and relocating yourself in time and space, in relationship to others and to your environment. You are the observer, living on the finite island of your individual self, looking out at a world of people and objects and places that is separate from and external to you. But when you let go of time and mind and world, and fall into the depths of consciousness itself, suddenly that observer who appeared to be finite stumbles upon that which is infinite. It's like stepping off a cliff into empty space. You lose all reference points, because your attention is on something that is not an object and that ultimately, in the shocking clarity of enlightened awareness, is revealed to be not separate from the one who is observing it. The separate self dissolves, the world dissolves, time and space seem to collapse. *The observer and the observed are one and the same.*

You are no longer a finite entity located at a fixed point in space and time, related to other objects that exist independently of you. You no longer experience yourself as existing at any particular point in space, because you have become one with the space itself. When the barriers between self and world dissolve in this way, you experience transparency. You won't feel that you are standing in any place, observing any thing. You won't know where you begin and where you end, where the back is or where the front is. This is what is traditionally called *nonduality.*

⊕

NONDUALITY MEANS "not two" or, more simply, it means that there is only One. Why do we use the term "nonduality"? Because it's the most precise description of that mysterious singularity that is almost impossible to put into words. The term "One" leaves room for the possibility of another. But in the singularity of consciousness there is no other. It is "One without a second." Consciousness is that One which is never two.

So what does nonduality actually mean? It means that your experience of your deepest self and my experience of my deepest self and any other human being's experience of his or her deepest sense of self is *One*. It's one and the same self. The journey back to before the beginning is a journey from the many to the One. This is the mystical paradox: that there seem to be many, but there is, in fact, only One. You and I may appear to be at two different points in space. But my deepest self and your deepest self are the same self. At that ground of deepest subjectivity, or interiority, we are not separate. The *interior* of all things is One. The inside of the cosmos is One. You may seem to be sitting there reading this book. I may seem to be far away. But when you follow these words back to before the beginning of time, to the innermost dimension of all things, what you experience as your deepest self is exactly the same self that I experience. We end up in the very same place. In that interior dimension, there is no *here* and no *there*, no you and no me. There is only the Self.

As you contemplate the nature of consciousness and you awaken to this pure subjectivity in your own awareness, ask yourself: Could there be anyone else here? Is there another? Could there ever be anything separate from this One Self? If you really go into it, you will find the answer. If you go all the way back to before the beginning—before thought, before feeling, before your body or your mind, before the world and the whole universe was created—what is there? There is only you, and you are everything.

That is the freedom you taste in the ground of Being: the nature of consciousness before there was even the notion of an *other*. Before otherness, before there were two, there could be no relatedness, or any of the complexity that relatedness creates. And so there was only freedom—the inherent liberation of consciousness before it located itself in time and in space, as you or as me.

You see, the instant consciousness locates itself in a particular time and place, as a particular entity, it loses awareness of its inherent freedom. This is why we so often feel trapped. When the self is not enlightened, it is fundamentally identified with the notion of difference, unaware of its primordial unity.

Why do some of us mysteriously begin to yearn for spiritual liberation or enlightenment? Why do we seek? Why do we pray? Why do we meditate?

Because consciousness longs to be free.

The liberating experience of self-discovery that you feel when you awaken to the ground of Being is consciousness reawakening to the perennial truth that it is only One, that it is *not two*. The question *Who Am I?* dissolves in the recognition that *I AM*. This is the essence of the discovery of enlightenment—when you find what you are seeking for, you discover that it was always already the case. IT simply is … and I AM THAT.

THE SECRET OF ENLIGHTENMENT IS THE ABSOLUTE, unequivocal conviction that *it exists.*

What does that mean? It means you have discovered an unshakable confidence in the *fact* of nonduality—in the perennial mystical revelation that *IT IS … and I AM THAT.* A confidence in that which can never be seen or known is the very ground of the enlightened state. Being is ungraspable, it's unknowable, it's ever elusive, and yet it is the only place you can find true confidence in life. Why? Because it is the very Source of life itself.

The conscious experience of Being, which is what enlightenment is, has always been the ultimate answer to the most fundamental spiritual questions: *Who am I?* and *Why am I here?* Those who have tasted enlightened awareness find that in that experience, any trace of existential doubt and all the questions that go along with it instantaneously disappear. It's not even that they are answered, but rather, the questions lose their meaning. When you locate the nonrelative, or absolute, nature of consciousness in the depths of your own self, it is experienced as a clarity that is empty of content; a weightiness that is full of nothing in particular; a profound knowing that dissolves all questions. In that questionless state, you find yourself profoundly rooted and radically free, supported by an absolute confidence in the knowing of no-thing that changes everything. The experience of that empty ground *is* the answer—the one answer that always liberates each and every one of us. You simply know, unequivocally, before thought, that *I am.* That's the only answer: I AM. There is no why.

# CHAPTER 3

# We Were There When It All Began

WHEN YOU HAVE JOURNEYED all the way back to before the beginning, and come to rest in the empty void before the universe was born, it can seem like the end of the path. Where else could there possibly be for you to go? The very notion of seeking for liberation, for enlightenment, for meaning or purpose seems absurd. The question *Who am I?* is answered before it is asked. And the question *Why am I here?* simply does not arise.

In traditional enlightenment, this is the end of the path. But the journey of *Evolutionary* Enlightenment does not end here. Why? Because the cosmic experiment that is life did not end here. If that empty ground, where every question is answered, was all there was to know and to discover, why would the universe exist? *Why did something come from nothing?*

Think about this for yourself: In the experience of the ground of Being, as you have discovered for yourself, there is no desire to *do* anything, no impetus whatsoever. There is nothing to do, nowhere to go, and no one to be or become. That's what it was like before the universe was born, remember?

And yet, here we are. Out of that utter peace, from the depths of that desirelessness, for some reason this miraculous process burst forth. Why? Why *did* something come from nothing?

This is not an abstract philosophical question but a profound spiritual contemplation that can take you to the essence of what it means to be alive. Why *did* something come from nothing ... and become light, energy, matter, life, consciousness, and *you*—fourteen billion years later reading these words? *Why are you here?*

If the eternal perfection that is the Source of everything knows no desire, why would the universe have emerged? If the ground of all things has no impulse but to *be*, why did it *become?* But it did. And thanks to evolutionary science, we can behold just how far this miraculous explosion of Becoming has brought us in the fourteen billion years since that initial burst. We can reflect on its awe-inspiring progress, and wonder at its ever-greater complexity and integration and creativity. And we can ask ourselves, why did all of this come from nothing?

I believe that for a human being today who aspires to find enlightenment, that question is an essential part of awakening. It is not enough to follow the question *Who am I?* to that timeless place where all questions dissolve. We also need to know: *Why am I here?* And to find the answer to *Why am I here?*, understanding the primordial moment when something came from nothing is crucial. We need to know what actually happened at the very beginning, at that instant when Being gave rise to Becoming.

When I ask this question, I'm not just talking about whether you believe in a biblical God or a big bang, or a whole series of cosmic explosions. I'm talking about a different kind of knowing—a direct, experiential recognition of what occurred in that moment fourteen billion years ago. You don't need a powerful telescope to see all the way back to the big bang—you can *go there*, right now, in your very own experience.

SCIENTISTS LOOK AT THE BIG BANG from the outside, so to speak, using complex instruments and the laws of physics to show us the explosion of light and energy, which became matter, which, in turn, gave rise to life, from which emerged the capacity for consciousness. But the perspective I'm sharing with you is one that looks at that very same event from the *inside*—that gets right beneath the surface of the stillness before the beginning, and locates the very impetus behind that primordial moment of birth.

You see, the big bang is not just a metaphor or a disputed scientific theory about what occurred fourteen billion years ago. It's happening *right now*. Something is coming from nothing every second. You might not be conscious of it, but it's true. Your own experience of action and reaction is not unbroken—there are countless moments of zero between each and every thought, every impulse, and every response. Something is coming from nothing, in and through each and every one of us, constantly. If you slow your experience down, and keep slowing it down, you'll start to see that there is a vast chasm of empty space that is the foundation of everything that is occurring, the ground out of which each impulse arises. Even as you are aware of the body, of the passing of time and the movement of thought, beneath it all you can become conscious of this current of stillness that is the ground of Being.

Because you can locate that empty ground in your very own experience, you can also locate the seed of everything that came out of that nothingness. When you contemplate the ground of your own Being, you can begin to intuit for yourself what that very moment when something came from nothing must have been like.

LET YOURSELF SINK, ONCE AGAIN, into that place before the beginning. What could be more still or peaceful than that empty ground? Absolutely nothing has yet occurred. When you rest in that deepest dimension of yourself, you experience a peace that is absolute. There is a miraculous quality to it, because it is infinitely deeper than any experience of peace, tranquility, or contentment that you could imagine with the mind. This is what it must have been like before the universe was created.

In that emptiness, you experience two things. First, there is unconditional freedom, which is the inherent quality of consciousness when it is unencumbered by attraction to anything other than itself. But also, in that empty no-place, there is something else.

If you pay close attention to your own experience, you will begin to realize that there is more to nothingness than meets the eye. The nothingness is not nothing. Nothing is *happening* there, and yet it is deeply compelling. If you get into a deep state of meditation it's absolutely enthralling. There is *something* in the nothingness that, once discovered, is absolutely absorbing.

In that unmanifest domain, nothing has happened yet … but *everything is possible.* Everything came from that no-place! So even in the absolute nothingness prior to the big bang the *potential* for everything must have existed. That is what captivates your attention as you rest in that empty stillness—the sense of *infinite potential*. It is experienced as a suspended state of absolute awakeness, a quiet tension that exists in consciousness because everything is possible.

*Everything is possible, but nothing has yet occurred*—that is the vibration in the ground of Being, dancing just below the surface. That's what you begin to feel when you put your attention on the moment when the universe was born.

THE ESSENCE OF THE NEW ENLIGHTENMENT, which I call Evolutionary Enlightenment, is found in that precise moment when nothing became something. This is the revelation that liberates: that *in
your very own experience* you can find that same vibration—the same
energy, the creative tension that initiated the entire process at the very
beginning.

Who or what was it that initiated this process? What energy or
intelligence made the choice to take the miraculous leap from formlessness to form? When you experience that vibration for yourself,
you know without a doubt that the birth of the universe could not
have been an accident, a random mechanical act. Somewhere, some-
how, a choice must have been made. This is why I use the term God
to represent *whoever or whatever made that choice.* That creative principle, that initial impulse to *become,* could only have been generated by
an energy or intelligence that is nothing less than godlike. So in the
way that I am using the term, God is not "out there," somewhere up
in the sky. God represents the creative principle, the First Cause, or
Eros, the elemental driving force behind the evolving universe. God
is what I call the "evolutionary impulse"—that overwhelming urge
to Become that emerges from the deepest dimension of Being itself,
which of course, is not separate from your very own consciousness.

That is why we could say that at the very beginning, at the
moment when the initial leap from formlessness to form took place,
*you and I were there.* Think about it for a moment.

*Is there anywhere else that you could have been at the moment when the
universe was born?*

We are told that all matter, time, and space was once a great
singularity—compressed into one fine point. When something came
from nothing, that one point was the only place to be. So we were *all*
there. *We* were there ... but we were there as *I*. Before the universe

was born, the One had not yet become the many. So there was only You, and You were alone.

And since you were the only one, the only reasonable conclusion is that *you* made that choice to do this. *To create the universe. As* that creative principle, you/we/I *chose* to take form.

⊕

LET YOURSELF FOLLOW THIS THEOLOGICAL FANTASY, just for a moment. Imagine what it would be like to be God, resting in a perfectly blissful, overwhelmingly peaceful state of being for infinite eons of no-time. In that profound stillness, nothing is missing, and there is no desire whatsoever. Absolutely nothing has occurred. That's where you were before the beginning, before the big bang. Perfect peace and boundless bliss. Quietude without end. Unburdened by the weight of existence, you could not have been more content.

Yet, for some reason, out of that perfect contentment, you made a decision to create the cosmos. You chose to manifest a material universe from your own unmanifest emptiness. You could have continued to rest happily in Being, meditating on nothingness for more countless eons of infinite no-time. But you had already done that—forever! So you chose to take the unthinkable step and endeavor to manifest your own self in and through form.

Where did that choice come from? Where, in that empty perfection, would the impetus arise to do something so vast, so complex, so overwhelming? What could be a greater challenge than to create something out of nothing, to manifest a material universe *before form had ever existed?*

But you apparently decided to take that unimaginable step.

How do I know? *Because it's happening.* Because we are here, now, fourteen billion years later, reflecting on this very question.

And considering the fact that at the deepest level of consciousness itself, there is only One, and that One is who you always are, you would have to conclude that at every step of the way—from before the beginning in infinite no-time, through the choice to take the plunge from formlessness into form, and up until the present moment—it could only be you and you alone who is responsible for all of this.

Who else could it possibly be?

## CHAPTER 4

# A Big Yes

OUR JOURNEY HAS TAKEN US ALL THE WAY BACK to the empty ground before time began, and inside the very birth of everything. We were there, remember? When you realize that you have been here since that very first moment, your whole perspective expands to unimaginable proportions. Your most fundamental beliefs and convictions about life are called into question, because suddenly the term "life" has taken on a whole new meaning.

When we think about life, we usually mean "*my* life"—a few decades of personal history, a particular circle of family and friends, within a certain culture. We don't think of a fourteen-billion-year process of evolution and development that burst out of nothing and became the entire cosmos. But *that's* life. And the experience you are having in this moment, as you are breathing in and out, as you read these words, is all part of life in the biggest sense, part of one inconceivable, vast, integrated process. The life I'm speaking about *is* the something that came from nothing, and that is who and what you are. That which burst into being fourteen billion years ago has become *you*. And you were also the one who set all of it in motion— who made the momentous decision to take that unimaginable leap from formlessness to form. *That's* why you are here.

If you have glimpsed this truth, even for the briefest of moments, it can call into question convictions you may not even know you hold. How do you really feel about *life?* Be honest with yourself. You may find that deep down you are not convinced that life is a good thing. For too many of us who have grown up in a secular, materialist society, life is a shallow, limited event, disconnected from both the boundless depths of Being and the vastness of Becoming. Isn't that why you are seeking spiritual enlightenment in the first place—as a way to escape from the apparent meaninglessness of existence, from the suffering and confusion that define "your life"?

But in light of what you have realized, that conclusion doesn't make sense any more. If you were there when it all began, then "your life" can no longer be limited to your brief human lifespan or your particular personal history. The suffering and confusion of your personal self no longer defines who you are. Your identity is not separate from the very Source itself, or from everything that sprang from that Source. You are the empty ground out of which everything emerged. And you are also the *evolutionary impulse*—the urge to become, the desire to exist.

From that newly awakened perspective and self-sense, you need to reexamine your deepest assumptions about life, to ask yourself the most fundamental question: What is the ultimate nature of life itself? *Is life inherently good?* When something came from nothing, when the universe burst into being fourteen billion years ago, was that a positive event? Was it a terrible mistake? Or was it a meaningless accident?

One way I like to approach this question is: When something came from nothing, was it a big YES? A big NO? Or a big NEUTRAL?

THIS IS NOT JUST AN ENTERTAINING thought experiment. You may never have consciously considered this question before, but you already have an answer. Your culture and your personal life experience have predisposed you to see life in one of these three ways. How you have unconsciously answered this question is *already* affecting the way you relate to life at the most fundamental level, and it shapes your spiritual aspirations as well. The way we think about life is the foundation stone and the expression of our worldviews, our cultures, and our spiritual traditions.

Look into this question seriously for yourself, considering all three of the possibilities. First, is life a negative event? Was the big bang a big "No"? That may sound absurd, but it's not an uncommon way to think. Are you deeply convinced that this world is a good place to be? Or do you find yourself seeking escape? Do you secretly long for transcendence, for release from a life full of confusion and suffering? You may make the best of it, and even endeavor to alleviate that suffering for yourself and others, but still deeply cherish the conviction that this world is not a good place. And you would not be alone in that conviction. Indeed, many of the great religious traditions, both East and West, are built on such a worldview. The first of Buddhism's Four Noble Truths tells us that "life is suffering." The Bible tells us that we are sinners in a world of temptation. In these, and many other religious worldviews, the ultimate goal of spiritual striving is to escape from this world, to find liberation, enlightenment, or salvation in a transcendent state or a heavenly realm. When the goal of a spiritual path is to escape from this world, the implicit message is that being here is not a good thing. Many of the great traditions, and many of today's spiritual seekers, still have this kind of subtle or not-so-subtle otherworldly bias, which by implication means that this world is not *it*. So if you long for transcendence, heaven, or eternal peace, you need to ask yourself, what does that mean about my relationship to *this* world?

The second possibility is that life is neither good nor bad. The big bang was one big … neutral. Perhaps this was all a meaningless cosmic accident, a random event that just happened to occur fourteen billion years ago, and has been unfolding mechanically ever since. Do you believe the life-process has inherent meaning? Or do you see it as merely a material event—scientifically fascinating and full of mysterious and complex systems but devoid of any deeper purpose or direction? With the ascendance of scientific materialism and secularism in our culture, this orientation to life is more and more common. In fact, it is considered by some to be the most evolved, sophisticated perspective. Scientific materialism tells us there is no inherent meaning in the act of creation. It's just happening. We live in a meaningless and purposeless universe. We can choose to *give* it meaning, but the unfolding of life is ultimately nothing more than a mechanical and biological process. If you are convinced that life is neutral and meaningless, what does *that* mean about your relationship to being here?

The third possibility is that life is inherently good. What does that mean? It means that the big bang was a big, resounding YES! When all manifestation burst into being out of nothingness, it was an inconceivably positive event, an expression of profound goodness. Could you accept that *life is good* at such a fundamental level? That doesn't necessarily mean that everything that happens *in life* is good. Of course, many things occur within the process that are tragic, painful, senseless, and even evil. Nature can be brutal and violent. Life includes hurricanes, earthquakes, wars, and deadly diseases. But some of the people who have most deeply contemplated the story of life's cosmic deep-time unfolding—from its explosive birth to this very moment—have come to the conclusion that the essence of the process is fundamentally good. When you understand the incredible delicacy of each pivotal point, and glimpse what it has taken for evolution to bring us to this place, you may find yourself awestruck by the miracle of life itself—its creativity, its tenacity, its extraordinary potential. There can be intimations of an overwhelming goodness—God's uncontainable, inconceivable YES—that underlies everything, a fundamental positivity that is almost impossible for the human mind to comprehend. If you are convinced that this is the ultimate nature of life, then what does *that* mean about your relationship to being here?

IT'S VERY IMPORTANT TO LOOK into this profound question for yourself: *What is the ultimate nature of life?* Why is it important? Because it affects everything. When you or I have a bad day, it's essential to be clear about whether that bad day is occurring in an ultimate context that is inherently good, or that bad day is occurring within a meaningless cosmic accident, or that bad day is occurring within a vast and seemingly endless nightmare.

If you are convinced the life-process is negative, then it makes sense to want to escape from it as quickly as possible. In the time when many of the great ascetic traditions were born, it's understandable that people would have felt this way. Imagine living in a world where you didn't know about the miracle of the evolutionary process. Imagine that life was short, brutal, and more often than not spent struggling just to survive. It would make sense to see the world as an endless cycle of birth, suffering, death, and rebirth, from which the only escape was through transcendence. It would make sense to long for a heavenly realm if you had not yet discovered that the world of time and form and becoming was *going somewhere*. But even though we now live in a very different world, and we now know that this vast process is going somewhere, the conviction that life is negative can still persist. If this is what you believe, it will profoundly color your relationship to life. And your own suffering or struggle will only serve to confirm that fundamental conviction.

If you are convinced that the process is meaningless, that too will deeply shape your relationship to life. Cynicism and even nihilism will find a foothold in your soul, and spiritual depth will be always obscured by the seemingly impermeable surfaces of the material world. If this is your fundamental worldview, it makes sense that you might be living from one moment to the next, with little sense of overarching purpose. You might feel justified in simply trying to feel better and experience as much pleasure and satisfaction as you can. After all, what else would there be to do but to make the best you could of this meaningless event?

If you are convinced that the big bang was a big yes, you will find that your relationship to life is confronted with some very significant questions. After all, such a realization should be reflected in the way you relate to your own experience. If the life-process is an overwhelmingly positive event, and if the energy and intelligence behind that process is the most essential part of who we are, and its nature is fundamentally good, then we need to ask ourselves: Who are we to be depressed? Who are we to doubt? Who are we to be cynical? In the way I see it, if you know beyond any doubt that at its deepest level life is good, you should be committed to proving it through your own example. You have an obligation to demonstrate that primordial YES through your own confidence and unshakable conviction.

This perspective does not deny that life challenges us all, and we all have to suffer and struggle. But when we awaken to the inherent positivity that is driving the whole process, our relationship to our own suffering and struggle changes dramatically. Knowing that to exist is *good* will give you enormous soul-strength to bear the challenges that confront you and to live a dynamic and victorious life. It may not mean it's easy to be here. But you no longer expect that it should be. In fact, you feel the awakening of a sense of obligation to work as hard as you can to be an expression of the deep goodness you have seen.

When you think objectively about how much work went into creating your own capacity to have the experience you are having in this very moment—*fourteen billion years of hard work*—then it might even begin to strike you as immoral to spend too much time sitting around and worrying about the fears and desires of your personal ego. Surely the purpose of all that cosmic effort and creativity and positivity—from nothing to energy to light to matter to life to consciousness to *you*—could not possibly have been just for that. When you awaken to the evolutionary process and its endless creativity, and you discover how profound and complex the structure of our universe is, you start to recognize and appreciate, at a soul level, what a precious gift it is to *be here*.

MY OWN EXPERIENCE AND ONGOING INQUIRY has convinced me, beyond any doubt, that when something came from nothing it *was* a big YES—that the process itself is inherently, absolutely, and unconditionally positive beyond our mortal capacity to even begin to truly comprehend. And the reason I can say that, without hesitation, is that I have looked very deeply into this matter for myself.

But once again, you don't have to take my word for it. Why? Because you were there. If you want to know what the nature of that initial cosmic explosion was—and *is*—the answer is there to be found in your own deepest interior. And this teaching will show you how to discover that answer for yourself. As you will see, it is already present in your own experience. All you have to do is learn to recognize it.

## CHAPTER 5

# Awakening to Evolution

LET'S RETURN TO THAT PRIMORDIAL IMPULSE, that moment of choice. You don't have to go back fourteen billion years to locate it—that choice is happening all the time. It is the impulse to *become,* the desire to exist, the evolutionary impulse itself.

The evolutionary impulse is the consciously experienced choice-in-action to take form and become the whole universe. It is the energy and intelligence that burst out of nothing, the driving impetus behind the evolutionary process, from the big bang to the emerging edge of the future. And that impulse is active right now, throughout the life process, and at every level of your own human experience.

In fact, that life-pulsation is the most important part of who and what we are. When you locate that impulse in the depths of your own self, you will become aware that it is inherently free and explosive in its freedom. It is dynamic and completely unrestrained in its nature. While Being feels like eternal peace, Becoming feels completely different. The evolutionary impulse is felt as a sense of tremendous urgency, an *ecstatic* urgency. At the level of consciousness, it is experienced as a sense that something unthinkably important *must occur NOW.*

THE EASIEST PLACE TO LOCATE the evolutionary impulse is at the most basic level of your being: the physical body. In the body, the desire to *create form* is expressed as the sexual impulse—the biological imperative to procreate. It's the most elemental expression of the First Cause, or the big bang. That's why it's so powerful! When we experience the sexual impulse, we are feeling that very same vibration that released the enormous energy of the entire cosmic process, pulsating in our own bodies and minds.

If you observe the arising of sexual desire in your own experience, and pay attention to the impulse itself, rather than the particular individual or circumstances that aroused it, you can identify the qualities of the initial burst of cosmic becoming. You will experience that ecstatic urgency—a feeling of overwhelming positivity and the simultaneous sense that "I *must* ..."

At the physical level, all living creatures experience this creative impulse—that's how the life-process ensures its own continuation. But the sexual impulse is the most basic and least refined manifestation of that primordial vibration. Human beings also experience that impulse at higher levels of the self. Our miraculous propensity to *innovate,* to give rise to that which is new, is what makes us distinct from all other forms of life. Beyond basic survival needs, no other life form seems compelled to innovate in this way. But human beings are driven by an innate creativity that expresses itself in art, science, technology, and beyond. What drives this ever-accelerating change and innovation that characterizes human culture? It is that same energy and intelligence that initiated the entire evolutionary process. What does it feel like? Ecstasy and urgency.

Think about your experience of those moments when you are most creatively engaged. What does it feel like? Being in a creative "flow" can be ecstatic and, simultaneously, there is an often surprising sense of urgency to bring into being that which you can sense is possible. That's why great artists or scientists will work day and night, neglecting to eat or sleep. They are driven by a vision, something just beyond their reach that will not let them rest until they have brought it into reality. That drive is the very same impetus that caused the whole universe to burst forth, fourteen billion years ago, and is now expressing itself through the body, mind, heart, and talents of an inspired human being.

When you feel that creative flow, often you discover a part of yourself you are not normally aware of, but which feels more like your "self" than the person you usually think you are. It's like plugging in to a deeper source of energy and passion that transcends whatever limitations you ordinarily assume. A deeper, more authentic part of your self is creatively released. That's why such moments are so fulfilling—it's not just the creative work you produce, but the experience of being more alive, more connected, more in touch with a sense of meaning and purpose.

The expression of the evolutionary impulse as human creativity and innovation is a unique and miraculous emergence in the unfolding of the cosmos. But there is an even higher expression of that impulse that some human beings feel awakening in their own hearts and minds. At the highest level, the evolutionary impulse is experienced as the spiritual impulse, the mysterious compulsion to *become more conscious.* Sometimes we feel this as an inexplicable yearning, a reaching toward perfection. At other times, it's a nagging and relentless existential discomfort, a sense that I *must* find a way to wake up, to evolve, to liberate my heart and enlighten my mind. This spiritual longing, this ecstatic urge to *become more conscious,* is the most profound expression of that initial cosmic explosion.

*Your own spiritual yearning is not separate from the big bang itself.*

The spiritual impulse is that very same intention that forged the cosmos out of nothing, that drives us to procreate, that inspires us to innovate and create that which is new. But at this highest level, the instrument of our creativity is not matter or flesh, nor a canvas or violin. Our very own consciousness, our deepest self, becomes the instrument through which the original evolutionary impulse strives to express itself and to fulfill its insatiable desire to *become*.

Think about that for a moment. Your spiritual longing may *seem* like your personal desire, but is it really? Could there really be anything personal about that pure, passionate aspiration to awaken, to become, to evolve? The entire universe, including your own experience in this very moment, is the expression and manifestation of that one desire.

THIS SINGULAR EVOLUTIONARY IMPERATIVE is inherent in the fabric of the entire cosmic process—from the big bang to the present moment. It has been here at every step, through each slow mutation and in each momentous leap. And as that impulse, you have also been here. We have *all* been here, throughout the mind-opening, awe-inspiring journey of Becoming that has been unfolding since time began. We've been together since infinite density emerged from absolute nothingness. We've been together since atoms, which make up the very foundation of all matter, were formed three hundred thousand years later. We were there when those atoms formed gas clouds, which turned into stars, which grouped together as galaxies, each of which eventually produced billions of solar systems filled with small rocky planets, such as our beautiful Earth, which was forged from the remains of generations of dead stars.

We have been here since the first single-celled microorganisms emerged from the primordial soup and throughout the slow flowering of life in all its diversity. We were here when the great dinosaurs ruled the food chain unchallenged, and through their demise. When the first hominids walked on the African savannah, this impulse, which is who we all are, guided each evolutionary step. And since our ancestors appeared on the stage of life just two hundred thousand years ago, that impulse has guided the vast unfolding tapestry of cultural development that brings us to this present moment.

Throughout this whole process, from the beginning of time to the very edge of the future, as the energy and intelligence that has been driving cosmic, planetary, biospheric, animal, human, and cultural evolution, we have been here. As the *evolutionary impulse*, as the initiatory force that is driving the entire creative process, from the innermost dimensions of our human interiors all the way to the farthest reaches of our cosmos, we have always been here.

AND THERE'S EVEN MORE TO IT than that. Not only were you here from the very beginning, but your own emotional, psychological, and spiritual experience, in the present moment, is the very furthest reaches of the evolution of the interior of the cosmos. This is not just an inspirational metaphor; it's literally true. When you awaken to the evolutionary impulse, you begin to live in the knowledge, awareness, and understanding of this fact every single day. You realize your own experience of consciousness itself from one moment to another is potentially the leading edge of the possible. Why? Because unlike all other forms of life on Earth, we play a unique role in the unfolding of that original impulse. While all forms of life, to differing degrees, have consciousness, *only human beings have the miraculous capacity to be aware of consciousness itself.*

As human beings, we *know that we know.* This capacity for self-reflective awareness, or self-consciousness, in the context of fourteen billion years of development, is a very recent emergence. And it means *everything.*

Because of the gift of self-reflective awareness, the human being, distinct from all other forms of life, has the capacity to recognize his or her own true identity as being *not separate* from the whole event of creation. Not separate from the ground of Being, the void out of which the universe emerged, and simultaneously not separate from the First Cause, from the big bang itself. And as we awaken to that surging energy and intelligence, *it* is just beginning to become aware of itself directly—through us. The human vehicle becomes a vessel through which the whole universe is able to know itself. Indeed, as far as we know, the energy and intelligence that created the universe is *only* able to know itself directly through the awakening human.

Could that energy and intelligence become aware of itself through a rock? A flower? A worm? A honeybee? A dog or a cat? If you think about it, it becomes obvious. Only human consciousness, as far as we know, has the unique quality of self-reflectivity that can enable God, or the energy and intelligence that initiated the creative process, to know him, her, or itself.

So the awakening of the spiritual impulse in the human heart and mind is the universe becoming conscious of itself through its own emerging creative process. When you—an awakening human being—experience that urge, the intensity of your creative inspiration is coming from the First Cause itself. The interior of the cosmos is awakening to itself within you, and responding to its own highest aspiration, *which is to become more conscious*. It's quite profound. Especially considering that it's taken fourteen billion years for evolution to bring life to the point where this was possible.

AS YOU AWAKEN TO THE SPIRITUAL IMPULSE, you begin to intuit and feel directly connected to the evolutionary momentum of the cosmos, to that surging energy and intelligence at the heart of life. You actually feel it working in you, moving in and through your body and mind as the mysterious compulsion to evolve at the highest level. This experience is the most subtle and profound expression of the initial cosmic explosion—the outer reaches of the big bang. That's the furthest it has gone, as far as we know right now: when *you*, a human being at the leading edge of this entire process, awaken to this mysterious compulsion to evolve at the level of your very own consciousness. The spiritual impulse *is* the experience of the big bang as a surging compulsion for interior development and growth. The innermost regions of the cosmos are aspiring to evolve and be developed in and through you.

Can you recognize how absolutely meaningful your own aspiration to awaken is? Do you see the precious significance of even the barest murmurings of your own struggle to become more conscious?

# CHAPTER 6

# The Universe Project

WHEN YOU SAY YES to the impulse to evolve, you find yourself overwhelmed by profound positivity. Your whole being aligns with the inherent goodness of life, of consciousness, of knowing who you are, and the miraculous nature of the process you are part of. When you've awakened to this evolutionary impulse, you have no doubt that *it* is good, that life is good, that God is good, that the whole process is good. It is inherently good, and you know what? It *wants* to be better.

Of course it wants to be better—that's why you experience the evolutionary impulse! That's what the urge to evolve is all about, especially when that impulse becomes aware of itself through the awakening human being. Then you directly experience *how much* the process itself wants to evolve, wants to develop. The energy and intelligence that initiated the big bang is compelling *you*, as its own creation, to evolve. Why? Because to whatever degree you evolve, that very energy and intelligence evolves also. If that impulse is what God is, in the manifest realm, then *God evolves through you*—through each and every one of us, *as* we evolve. When you really get this, there's only one thing left to do: you have to get on with it. You have to evolve, you have to develop, you have to *become.* This is when God's purpose becomes your purpose.

What is God's purpose? To create the universe, in his or her own image. And what is that image? *Consciousness.* To create a material universe in the image of God, as outrageous as it sounds, means nothing less than the awakening or enlightenment of all matter. This seemingly impossible task is what I call the Universe Project.

From this perspective, we've obviously barely begun. It's been fourteen billion long years, which to the human mind is an inconceivably vast expanse of time, but in the mind of God is probably just a few moments, considering what an infinite project this process appears to be. So the creative principle, the God-impulse, has an overwhelming amount of work to do.

Throughout history, when we've been in need, we've prayed to God for help. But now, at the beginning of the twenty-first century, God needs *our* help. The fact that highly evolved beings can now awaken directly to the evolutionary impulse means that God, as the creative principle, is able to see, hear, taste, touch, and feel like never before his or her own creation, through *us.* And even more importantly, that cosmic intelligence and creative energy can begin to *consciously act* through the awakened human being.

If that principle is who and what we really are, if we have recognized that I Am That—the *acting* representative of the creative principle in the world—then what we are doing, and *why* we are doing it, becomes all important. God is dependent upon *us.* Indeed, the evolution of consciousness, which is the evolution of the interior of the cosmos, is entirely dependent upon the conscious evolution of human beings at the leading edge. There is no other way for God, that primordial energy and intelligence, to evolve in and through matter.

WHAT DOES IT MEAN TO EMBRACE God's purpose as your own? Where can you find the energy, the commitment, the courage to embrace something that vast?

It already exists within you.

Remember, the evolutionary impulse *is* your own desire to develop. And that part of you is the energy and intelligence behind the evolving universe. It never rests. It's a ceaseless, endless reservoir of energy, passion, and awakened care. Care for what? For the future.

For that dynamic impulse, there is only the unmanifest promise of the next moment. The evolutionary impulse is never concerned with the present moment, however significant it may appear to be. Why? Because the present moment has already happened, so there is not much that we can do about it. We've already arrived there. But the future, which always exists in the next moment, and the next, is something we *can* impact. So the eternal passion of the evolutionary impulse is *change.* It is always only interested in the future, always one step ahead, ever reaching for what's on the edge of the possible.

Much of mysticism, both ancient and contemporary, is focused on the present. "Be here now," we are told. "Be in the moment." And while that may bring some release and relief in the short term, in an evolutionary context you discover that the present isn't where the action is. The action is in the future, because the future is something that you can get involved in creating. The future is something that you can take responsibility for in the most exciting way possible. When you begin to care about evolution, you awaken to a passion for the future that is all-consuming.

When you experience the evolutionary impulse moving within you, you will feel an unbelievable excitement and thrill about life, because of what you can *create.* That's what you thrive on, it's what excites you, it's what lights up your heart and mind: the creative potential for building the future that exists in the present moment. And that inexhaustible thrill is not separate from the impulse that initiated this entire creative process out of nothing fourteen billion years ago.

AWAKENING TO THE EVOLUTIONARY IMPULSE is inherently liberating, because its nature is ecstatic, limitless freedom and boundless energy. But there is a price to be paid. In that freedom there is no rest, nor is there any peace.

The evolutionary impulse does not *need* to rest and has no interest in peace. Its passionate longing will never experience satisfaction. It's simply not capable of it. It is a function of consciousness, an impulse that is compelled to create the future, perpetually. Its nature is relentless creativity, and it is only interested in pulling the future into the present, ceaselessly striving to usher into existence that which has not yet emerged. And when that potential does begin to enter into actuality, that part of yourself experiences no relief whatsoever, because its attention is already on the next possibility, the next moment and the next, because that is its function, *forever*. The evolutionary impulse exists in a state of constant creative tension that is never released, always suspended between what is and what could be.

This is the paradox of the evolutionary impulse. Its very nature is a utopian idealism, an urge toward perfection, yet that perfection can never be realized in the manifest world. You are never going to reach perfection; I'm never going to reach perfection. Perfection isn't possible in the realm of time and form and becoming.

Before something burst out of nothing, before anything happened, we could say perfection existed. It exists in the realm of the unborn, unmanifest, *unbecome*, which is the ground of Being in every moment. But the minute you, as that original evolutionary impulse, decided to create the universe and took the leap from formlessness to form, perfection was left behind. And the whole creative process can be understood as the eternal striving for a perfection that can never be reached. The entire cosmos is endlessly reaching toward perfection but destined never to get there.

The evolutionary impulse is a force and function of nature that does not cater to our personal emotional and psychological needs—and yet it depends upon us to be vehicles for it to express itself in this world. For the finite, mortal human self, the raw, overwhelming, ceaseless, and perpetual nature of that urge always feels like too much to bear. But that's simply how it is—the evolutionary impulse is a higher dimension of an infinite process that includes our humanity but also transcends it. So as individuals, you and I need to cultivate incredible strength of character in order to bear that part of the self that transcends our human frailty. The evolutionary impulse in each and every one of us will always be too much and will never be satisfied.

To give ourselves wholeheartedly to the evolutionary impulse is the great sacrifice, the ultimate expression of surrender, because there is no end in sight. Whatever happens, as glorious as it may be, will never be enough. All we will ever know is that *so much more needs to happen*. Do you or I have the humility and awakened love in our hearts to give ourselves to that? For most of us, it's too much. An extraordinary degree of renunciation and courage is required to be a bearer of this powerful creative function as a human being. But as I understand it, this is what it truly means to live the spiritual life.

THE DYNAMIC, FUTURE-ORIENTED, ECSTATICALLY INSPIRED state of the evolutionary impulse *is* the new enlightenment that I am speaking about. The inner eye has become compelled by the ever-unfulfilled promise of creating the future at a higher level than what exists in the present moment. When the awakening to this powerful spiritual urgency becomes one's irrevocable attainment and permanent state, one has surely landed on the yonder shore, where the evolutionary impulse has become the driving force or fundamental principle guiding the vehicle called the body, mind, and soul.

This awakened passion for evolutionary transformation is not reasonable. It demands *change*, right now, and it will *not* wait, because God is always desperate to grow. God is infinite in the unmanifest realm. But in the manifest realm God is not infinite—God can only know him- or herself to the extent to which conscious beings are actually able to awaken to their own absolute nature. So the creative principle's desire to grow won't be satisfied until the whole universe has awakened to itself and to its absolute nature. When a human being awakens to the evolutionary impulse and experiences the urgency of that compulsion to evolve, that's what he or she is feeling—God's desperation. That's why it is not reasonable, and it never will be.

God is only as powerful *in this world* as those of us who have the courage and audacity to awaken in this way—to become one with our own impulse to evolve. That's the awesome significance of being a human being who is *awake*. When you realize this for yourself, you discover what an extraordinary blessing it is to be who you are, in this world, right now. In fact, the whole point of the creative process *is* to be here—to participate fully, radically, *consciously* in the Universe Project. In this evolutionary context, the point of enlightenment is not merely to transcend the world so that you can be free of it but to *embrace* the world completely, to embrace the entire process as your self, knowing that you are the creative principle incarnate, and *you* have a lot of work to do. As an individual, you are instantaneously liberated, simply through taking that step, but your personal liberation is a mere by-product of finally embracing the awe-inspiring burden of the Universe Project, which in truth has been yours all along.

YOU ARE THE ONLY ONE who can do this. That's the ultimately challenging and profoundly liberating truth you discover in Evolutionary Enlightenment. Any individual who is committed to this path has to know, at the deepest level, that he or she is *the only one who could possibly do this.* And that is because there is no other. You have discovered that fact, directly, for yourself. From the absolute or nondual perspective that emerges in spiritual revelation, there *is* only ONE. *There literally is no other;* there is only One without a second. To truly understand conscious evolution, you must grapple with the profound implications of that fact. I believe we can only consciously evolve to the degree that we have realized at the deepest level of our being that we *are* that One without a second.

In an evolutionary context, facing into the truth of nonduality—that the many is the One and that the One is ultimately who we always are—forces a confrontation with any relationship to the life process that is less than whole, complete, and fully committed. To consciously evolve is to surrender unconditionally to the truth that there is no other and at the same time to accept responsibility for what that means in an evolving universe—a cosmos that is slowly but surely becoming aware of itself through you and me. That One without a second is simultaneously awakening to itself as it develops, as it evolves, and it is that One, as you and me, alone, that can now begin to take responsibility for endeavoring to consciously create its own future.

Of course, in this manifest dimension, where the One is expressed through the many, those of us who have awakened to our responsibility for the process then begin to engage in this heroic endeavor *together*. But each individual has to be willing to be *the One*. This is the spiritual physics of Evolutionary Enlightenment. It works only if each one of us knows without a doubt that *I am solely responsible*. And nothing puts greater pressure on the separate self-sense than that.

The greatest challenge for a mortal human being is to realize and take responsibility for the fact that who you are right now, in all your imperfection, is that One without a second, and that One is endeavoring to develop and become more conscious as you. God has fallen out of the sky, but now he, she, or it is emerging as the spiritual impulse and longing to *consciously* evolve in, through, and *as you*.

So you must ask yourself: Do I have the guts, the audacity of intention, the boldness of spirit? Do I have enough love in my heart to be willing to be the One? The answer to that question is really the answer to every important question.

*Who am I?*

*Why am I here?*

*Is there a purpose to all this?*

All of these questions are answered in the deepest possible way when you point the finger at yourself and say "Yes."

**PART II**

# Understanding the Territory

# INTRODUCTION TO PART II

ANYONE WHO IS SERIOUS ABOUT embarking on the path of spiritual evolution must make the effort to acquaint themselves with the territory. The territory of Evolutionary Enlightenment is the interior of the cosmos. What is the interior of the cosmos? It is your very own experience of consciousness and cognition, right now. The exterior of the cosmos is matter; the interior is consciousness. So the territory is your own self, in the deepest sense of what that means—all the way from the radically impersonal depths of pure timeless Being to the complex workings of your ever-evolving individual self-sense.

Spiritual development, in the context of this teaching, is about compelling ourselves, through the power of our own inspired will and intention, to actually evolve. And in order to evolve—to *consciously* evolve—you first need to get to know the multidimensional nature of who you are and how you are. You need to be able to recognize and understand what constitutes your interior world—the infinite nature of the spiritual ground of your own being, the higher human capacities that make conscious evolution possible, and also the unconscious conditioned structures that can obstruct and obscure that potential. This is complex and subtle territory that is, for most of us, relatively unfamiliar. Indeed, it continues to surprise me how little most of us seem to know about ourselves—not only about our psychological interiors but also about the deeper dimensions of the internal universe.

In Part I of this book, we took a cosmic journey of awakening. In Part II, from the perspective of Evolutionary Enlightenment, we will examine the fundamental dimensions of the self, both relative and absolute; illuminate the unique challenges and potentials of the cultural context in which we find ourselves; and explore some of the higher human capacities that enable us to participate in such a bold and significant task as the evolution of the interior of the cosmos.

## CHAPTER 7

# The Self: Relative and Absolute

SPIRITUAL AWAKENING IS and always has been about self-discovery. Spiritual practice, to a large degree, is about learning to master the challenging art of differentiating between the many dimensions of your own self. This is no easy task. For all but the rarest among us, our sense of self, our experience of subjectivity, is so close to the eye of awareness that we find it difficult to gain enough distance to make these all-important and liberating distinctions. Indeed, although we experience our sense of self changing from one moment to another, we rarely understand what is actually happening.

When we experience deep states of meditation, for example, we may taste the primordial freedom of the timeless ground of Being, and find our sense of self engulfed in fathomless peace and bliss. In the same way, in moments of powerful spiritual inspiration, we may become so overwhelmed by the ecstatic urgency of the evolutionary impulse that we unselfconsciously experience that passion and energy as our own self. But sooner or later we may fall back into a more familiar, unenlightened, personal sense of identity. And throughout all of this, we are just aware of the rise and fall of different emotional, psychological, and spiritual states. What we do not realize is that *we are actually shifting between different dimensions of our own self.*

If we aspire to consciously evolve, it is essential that we cultivate an objective interest in who we are and how we are, and this kind of discrimination and self-inquiry requires spiritual inspiration and enormous effort. Without it, no matter what higher potentials we may awaken to, we will likely remain lost in the existential confusion and subjective drama of our ever-changing inner experience. I cannot overemphasize how important it is to know how to discriminate between the different dimensions of who we are. Even though we may be familiar conceptually with the internal universe, it is a rare individual who is spiritually developed enough to actually possess direct experiential knowledge of its multidimensional nature. And it is an even rarer individual who can navigate this challenging territory with the maturity of evolutionarily enlightened awareness.

TEACHINGS OF ENLIGHTENMENT, whether traditional or evolutionary, present us with a unique way of thinking about and understanding who we are. What makes an enlightened perspective different from any other perspective is that it emphasizes the significance of those dimensions of self that are non-relative, or "absolute."

What does "absolute" really mean, for human beings like you and me? For most of us who have grown up in a secular culture, almost every way we are accustomed to thinking about ourselves could be called relative. For example, we tend to think of ourselves as individuals with a unique personality based upon some combination of our psychological experience, our ethnic identity, our cultural background, our gender, and our personal strengths and talents. Some of us even base our fundamental sense of self on our shortcomings, weaknesses, or misfortunes. While these are real and valid aspects of ourselves, they are all relative because they are only partial. There is, however, another dimension altogether upon which we can base our sense of identity, a dimension that is radically different from all others because its very nature is non-relative or absolute. Absolute is a metaphor for that which is infinite, that which has no boundaries.

If the spiritual impulse has awakened within you, and you find yourself compelled to become an enlightened person, then it is the non-relative dimension of your self that you are most interested in. But if you are not deeply committed to your own enlightenment, then knowingly or unknowingly, you are going to be invested in a relative or partial definition of self. And most importantly, you are going to be convinced that that is the *whole* of who you are. Just imagine for a moment: Who would you be and how would you be if each and every relative expression of your self was recognized to be only a small *part* of an infinitely bigger picture?

IN TRADITIONAL ENLIGHTENMENT TEACHINGS, awakening to that which is absolute is what liberates us from the existential prison of the relative self, or ego. Now, ego is a tricky term, because it is used by many different people in many different ways to mean many different things. The way I talk about ego is very context-specific. There are many other ways to look at ego, and these are valid within their own contexts. For example, a psychologist's interest in what ego is and how it works comes from a very different perspective than that of a spiritual master. My interest in ego is context-specific, and that context is Evolutionary Enlightenment.

I use the word ego broadly to refer to *that which is an obstacle to our individual and collective potential to evolve*, that which is inhibiting our capacity to become enlightened men and women. And often, it is our conscious and unconscious attachment to different *relative* forms of self-identity that profoundly inhibits the process of spiritual evolution and enlightenment. So for the purposes of this discussion, we can say that "ego" is a shorthand for all the ways in which you are consciously and unconsciously identified with and attached to relative dimensions of self that are inhibiting your higher evolutionary development.

The question of what ego is remains a complex and subtle subject. But anyone who is interested in any kind of spiritual enlightenment, including Evolutionary Enlightenment, will become very interested in this particular dimension of the internal universe. Enlightenment always has been and always will be about evolution *beyond ego*. Most educated people are, at least to some degree, familiar with the term "ego" and some of its many definitions. But those of us who are deeply interested in spiritual enlightenment find this subject an ongoing source of profound fascination and contemplation. As this book continues to unfold, we will explore many of the different faces and facets of the ego, both individual and collective, as they reveal themselves in light of the aspiration to evolve.

You will only begin to appreciate how significant ego is in relationship to the seriousness of your spiritual aspiration to transcend it. Only to the extent that you have lived beyond the ego can you appreciate what an awesome obstacle it truly is. And the only reason I take ego so seriously is that the path and practice of Evolutionary Enlightenment is dedicated to creating a new world in the territory that lies beyond it.

To be clear, in this territory, the ego does not cease to exist altogether. But our conscious and unconscious investment in and attachment to those dimensions of the self that inhibit our evolutionary potential has been released. Once again, the way that this occurs is through the transformative awakening to a dimension of self that is absolute.

⊡

In Evolutionary Enlightenment, there are two ways that one can awaken to a dimension of self that is absolute.

As we explored in the opening chapters of this book, the first is found in the timeless, formless, primordial ground of Being. That deepest dimension of each and every one of us is what we discover when we have let go of thought, feeling, mind, time, and world. Remember, that is where we always were before the beginning, before the universe was born. The nature of the self, as timeless, formless Being, is experienced as radical, unconditional freedom. Freedom from being trapped in time and form—freedom from the mind and personality, freedom from everything that is relative, freedom from the whole world. That's why that deepest dimension of our own self is always so exquisite and delightful. Experiment with this radical release in the infinite depths of your own interior. *Give yourself the freedom to experience the unconditional freedom of Being.* Allow yourself to let go so deeply that you feel as if everything that happens within the realm of manifestation is incomparably mundane and even painful, in contrast to the profound lightness of being that is the deepest nature of your own unmanifest self.

When you awaken to your absolute identity in the depths of pure Being, there is always a distinctive quality of radical immediacy to its liberating nature. Because there is no time there, you don't have to work anything out or solve any particular problems before you can access its glory. That deepest dimension of yourself has *never been* trapped in any of your problems. The moment you experience this infinite empty ground, that liberating immediacy is always there.

Traditionally, this has been the source of enlightened awareness. Traditional enlightenment teachings call on us to transcend ego through shifting our deepest sense of identity to the Self Absolute that abides in and as the ground of Being. The foundation of Evolutionary Enlightenment is that same ground that is the final resting place and goal of traditional enlightenment.

But Evolutionary Enlightenment doesn't stop there. It asks you to take another leap and to embrace a very different shift of identity—one that is equally profound but much more relevant to the life-conditions in which we find ourselves today. This is where we discover another dimension of self that is *also* absolute. In the new enlightenment, we recognize that the evolutionary impulse or urge to Become is also an absolute, non-relative dimension of who and what we are. That impulse, as I have described, is nothing less than the energy and intelligence that initiated the creative process and is still driving it right now. And in the same way that the nature of your timeless, formless self is absolute, there is nothing relative or partial or less than infinite about the cosmic desire to exist in and through time and form.

Consider how this impulse manifests in your very own experience. It can be utterly overwhelming. The character of the evolutionary impulse is relentless ecstatic urgency. It is the non-relative Absolute expressed as an energetic compulsion to *become*. And it's a primordial drive that, once you awaken to it, will not leave you alone.

As I've previously described, you can locate this impulse at every level of the self—from the physical drive to procreate, to the creative compulsion to innovate, to the spiritual urge to evolve. When that impulse manifests in the human experience, as either an inspired act of creative genius or a surge of spiritually illuminated wisdom or insight, it temporarily *becomes* who you are—what I call the *Authentic Self* of the individual.

The purpose of this teaching is to create a receptivity within the self so that the evolutionary impulse can burst forth *as* who you are. And for this to happen, the ego must be displaced. In traditional mysticism, when the Absolute as the timeless, formless ground of Being, emerges in your experience, the ego falls into the background and what comes to the fore is infinite depth, overwhelming peace, inherent freedom, and profound clarity. In the same way, when you awaken to the Absolute as Eros, or the evolutionary impulse, the ego also falls into the background, but now what comes to the front is a liberated passion, fearlessness, courage, joy, and inspired readiness to evolve *now*. You directly experience your own self becoming a manifest expression of Eros in human form.

In the new enlightenment, when you undergo this kind of shift of identity, the ego is displaced to a significant degree by the evolutionary impulse, and you find yourself animated by that same inspired energy and intelligence that initiated the creative process. Your very self-sense becomes infused with that cosmic passion and purpose and the expression of your personality becomes illumined by that spiritually enlivened consciousness. The goal of Evolutionary Enlightenment is for that creative impulse to become *internalized,* so that it is not just a temporary experience or a momentary source of inspiration, but your *primary sense of self.* You become that and that becomes you.

Enlightened mystics bearing witness to the absolute nature of Spirit have long declared: "I Am That." In Evolutionary Enlightenment, as I've been describing, the "That" is not only the eternal ground of Being but *also* the evolutionary impulse. And it is the identification with That that awakens the Authentic Self and gives us the spiritual confidence and inspiration to do things we would otherwise not have the courage or audacity to do—too hemmed in by the inertia of our psychological fears and the unenlightened values and limiting perspectives of our shared culture.

Once again, the Authentic Self is the evolutionary impulse manifest in and through an individual who has freely, consciously chosen to identify with that *as self.* The Authentic Self is the evolutionarily enlightened self.

If you are evolutionarily enlightened it means that your ego—which once again means all the ways in which you are consciously and unconsciously identified with and attached to relative dimensions of your self that inhibit your higher development—has now been overshadowed by the blazing light of the evolutionary impulse. And this kind of awakening really does *change* who we are, because it transforms our deepest motivations.

When you are identified with the evolutionary impulse, with your own Authentic Self, you will find yourself in touch with a sense of *imminent*, infinite, immediate higher potential. And when you are flying on the wings of the Authentic Self, it literally feels like *anything is possible.* In those moments, the energy and intelligence that is driving the creative process comes alive in your own consciousness as the awareness of infinite potential.

The nature of the Authentic Self is always already spiritually motivated, turned on, tuned in, ready to respond to the radical immediacy of now. It experiences no fear, no doubt, no hesitation, no procrastination. Your Authentic Self is *always* already inspired and spiritually on fire. This is a new manifestation and expression of enlightened awareness.

Once again, traditional enlightenment is the experience of consciousness beyond ego that is the natural result of awakening to the timeless ground of Being. The new enlightenment is the experience of ego-transcendence carried on the wings of the evolutionary impulse.

## CHAPTER 8

# Enlightening the Choosing Faculty

HOW DO WE MAKE THE PROFOUND SHIFT from ego to Authentic Self? For most of us, it does not occur simply as a result of one flash of insight or revelation. On the contrary, making this shift usually requires inspired intention and consistent, diligent effort. And the way this is achieved is through using the greatest gift that evolution has given us: the power of choice.

The power of conscious choice, or free agency, is unique to human beings as far as we know. You and I are highly evolved individuated selves who have been blessed with the extraordinary capacity for self-reflective awareness and the freedom to choose. In fact, these are the very faculties that make it possible for us to consciously evolve. Think about it: You, whoever you are, at least to some degree have the power to choose. How much do you really appreciate the significance of this extraordinary birthright? It is surprising how few people consider the deeper implications of possessing the freedom to choose. Just imagine—without free agency, who would you be? Little more than a robot, unconsciously responding and reacting to conditioned egoic fears and desires, cultural triggers, biological impulses, and external stimuli, with no control over your own destiny. But while it is true that we are all profoundly influenced by many of these forces, both inner and outer, at the same time, it is equally true that we always have at least *some* measure of freedom to choose how we respond.

If you aspire to become an evolutionarily enlightened human being, your ability to do so depends upon accepting the simple fact that independent of external circumstances, *you always have a measure of freedom to choose.* That sounds like a simple statement, but it's amazing how many intelligent people will deny it. When you look honestly for yourself, however, you will see that it is true: you are *always* choosing. Sometimes your choices are conscious; sometimes they are unconscious. Sometimes they are inspired by the best parts of yourself; other times they are motivated by lower impulses and instincts. But the bottom line is that every time you act or react, at some level a choice is being made. And you, whoever you are, are the one who is making that choice. After all, who else could it be?

What I'm bringing to light here is an all-important function of the self that I call the "choosing faculty." This faculty is central to who and what each one of us is as a human being. In fact, when people ask me what the self is, I say that the self is the one who is making the choices. *You, whoever you are, are always choosing.* And what you choose to identify with, consciously or unconsciously, is always who and what you will become.

The path of Evolutionary Enlightenment is about consistently choosing to identify with your Authentic Self, rather than your ego. It's a simple concept to grasp, but not quite as simple to put into practice. Our freedom to choose is not unlimited. We each have *some measure* of freedom. Not complete freedom, but a measure, and that measure is greater for some people than it is for others. But as long as there is some it's enough to begin. If there is a measure of freedom then there *is* freedom to choose. And it is very important to understand that this choosing faculty alone is what makes conscious evolution possible.

You begin the path and practice of Evolutionary Enlightenment with the life-changing recognition of the power of your own choices. What that means is that in relationship to the important choices you make, you are never completely unconscious. There is always some degree of awareness, however small, which gives you the freedom to choose. And the path of conscious evolution is about increasing that degree of awareness, increasing that measure of freedom, until you are living as the enlightened self that you *consciously choose* to be, rather than the unenlightened self you have unconsciously and habitually identified with your entire life.

I believe that it *is* possible to take responsibility for the entirety of who you are in such a profound way that you can consciously choose who you want to be. But that doesn't mean it will be easy. The human self is by nature a complex multidimensional process, and within that process are many factors that limit our freedom and obscure our awareness. There are powerful biological instincts that still drive us on a deep level to act in ways that challenge our higher rational inclinations. There are all the karmic consequences of our personal history, the emotional and psychological tendencies that have formed in response to our particular life experience. There are layers of cultural conditioning, values and assumptions about how things *should* be that color our perspectives without us even knowing it. And many people believe that within our psyches we also carry the unresolved stories of previous lifetimes. All these factors play a part in the complex web of motives and impulses that makes up your sense of self. *All of this is you.* And yet it *is* possible to take responsibility for all of these dimensions of who you are, through the transformative recognition that *you are always the one who is choosing.*

ONE OF THE GREATEST CHALLENGES of the evolutionary process at all levels—from matter to life to consciousness—has to do with changing what have been called cosmic habits. A cosmic habit is simply a pattern formed by the way something has occurred many times in the past—at the level of matter, at the level of biology, or at the level of consciousness. For example, when matter has coalesced in a particular form over and over again, that form becomes a habit, that eventually contributes to determining the physical structures of our cosmos. When human beings take action in particular ways time and time again, those actions become habits that define the cultural structures of a tribe or nation. Similarly, when you as an individual repeat the same choices in relationship to your own mind and emotions, those choices also form habits that define your personality and your psychological self-sense.

The gradual formation and accumulation of habits is the process through which evolution unfolds and integrates at all levels. When something new is endeavoring to emerge, however, the old habits have to be broken. This is why, when you are trying to evolve at the level of consciousness, you have to deal with an enormous number of biological, emotional, psychological, and culturally inherited habits. These habitual responses and ways of feeling and thinking about yourself and the world are what you have to first and foremost make conscious, and when necessary, transcend, in order to make way for a higher expression of your own self to emerge. Until you make them conscious, those historical habits will inevitably determine who you identify yourself to be, and they will continue to drive the choices you make. Enormous effort, will-power, and intention will be required, especially at the beginning of the path, to break through these accumulated habits at all levels of your being. That's understandable—after all, they are the familiar ways that you have been responding to and engaging with the life process for your entire lifetime, and beyond.

The ego is, from a certain point of view, nothing more than a conglomeration of habits. There are emotional and psychological habits that create the personal ego, and there are cultural habits that create what I sometimes call the collective or cultural ego. They are all habits that have been useful for one reason or another in the past, but now, because you want to evolve, some of these ingrained tendencies can be recognized as obstacles to your higher development.

If you aspire to evolve, if you intend to become a conscious vehicle for the evolutionary impulse, you have to use the God-given powers of awareness and conscious choice to navigate between your new and higher spiritual aspirations, and all of the conditioned impulses and habits that are embedded in your self-system. You need to become so conscious that you can make choices that move you, consistently, in an evolutionary direction. And it is only through the wholehearted embrace of your power of choice that it becomes possible for you to do this.

This is what I often call "enlightening the choosing faculty"— bringing the light of consciousness, conscience, and higher purpose to bear on the unique and extraordinary capacity within that can define your destiny.

EVENTUALLY, IF YOU GO FAR ENOUGH in your spiritual development, the self-generated momentum of your own evolutionary choices will become the driving force of your life, rather than the unconscious habits of the past. And that's when something very profound occurs. Your capacity to choose will become more and more aligned with the creative freedom of the First Cause, the energy and intelligence behind the initial choice to become. When free agency, the greatest gift of the evolved human, is liberated from unconscious and habitual patterns and becomes identified with a higher or cosmic will, the individual becomes a conscious agent of evolution.

When your power of choice aligns itself with the evolutionary impulse in this way, your own deepest, heartfelt, spiritual aspiration becomes one with the original cosmic intention to create the universe. That's what Evolutionary Enlightenment is pointing to. To the degree to which you make conscious and transcend those outdated biological, psychological, and cultural habits within yourself that are inhibiting your higher development, you become an ever-more-powerful agent for conscious evolution.

Remember, we are all part of a deep-time developmental unfolding—each and every one of us, as awakening human beings. Our capacity for greater and greater consciousness and self-reflective awareness is the expression of a process that is perpetually awakening to itself. The capacity for freedom of choice is a relatively recent emergence in this process, and it grows and develops and increases according to how conscious and self-aware we become. As we evolve and develop and mature, as we liberate ourselves from our lower and more primitive impulses and habits, we become more and more conscious. And the more liberated our consciousness becomes, the more freedom we have to choose.

Transcending ego, in the way I've defined it, is critical for those of us at the leading edge of this vast process. Our psychological ego, by definition, keeps the context for our experience very small, fundamentally oriented around its personal fears and desires. Our culturally conditioned self-sense rarely sees beyond its own beliefs and values. If we refuse to authentically embrace a context that is bigger than the individual and collective ego, the true power inherent in the miraculous gift of choice is stifled by that narrow context. But when our free agency is liberated from the grip of ego, when the context for our choices expands to embrace the infinite depths of our cosmic identity, the choosing faculty becomes informed and enlightened by the limitless passion of the energy and intelligence that initiated the creative process. Then its transformative power is startling and profound. That's when you discover that free agency is potentially the most evolutionarily and spiritually significant aspect of your experience.

In this way, your power to choose becomes a function of the First Cause itself, endeavoring to create the universe at higher and higher levels, reaching for the very edge of the possible. And if you have the courage to go that far, you will begin to define what that edge actually is. When you get to that point where you are intentionally, deliberately, and actively participating in the process of evolution, you will find yourself pushing forward the creative potential of the interior of the cosmos, as a direct result of your very own choices. What could be a more sacred endeavor? Your choices enable consciousness to evolve. And when you are dedicated to that possibility, you are actually *compelling* it to do so. What an audacious thought: compelling consciousness to evolve.

Remember—evolution isn't just happening by itself. *We* are a very big part of that process. *You* are a very big part of that process. When you truly understand this, the liberation of the power of choice becomes the essence of the spiritual endeavor. You realize that the more awake you become, the more *enlightened* you become, the more responsible you are and the more profoundly significant are the choices that you make. In Evolutionary Enlightenment, we no longer ask God to save us; we step forward in the realization that *God is depending on us.* That's a very bold statement. But it's true. Hold up your hands. Whose hands are they? If you are identified primarily with ego, they are the hands of the ego, but if your purpose is fundamentally aligned with the creative principle, your hands become God's hands.

## CHAPTER 9

# The Postmodern Predicament

FROM THE PERSPECTIVE OF EVOLUTIONARY ENLIGHTENMENT, *you* are very important. Not your individual qualities, your unique personality, or your particular gifts and talents. What makes you important is that you have the extraordinary capacity to directly awaken to the fact that who you are is not separate from the energy and intelligence that created the universe. Even more significantly, you have the power to take responsibility for who you really are, if you *choose* to. In theological terms, this means that you can choose to become God—God as the creative principle.

Your human form and your sophisticated capacity for consciousness and cognition is, as far as we know, the highest expression of what the energy and intelligence that initiated the creative process has produced so far. This is where the entire fourteen-billion-year process has come: to you and me, the most complex forms of sentient life, with our miraculous faculties for self-reflective awareness and conscious choice. Remember, it is only through the awakening human, who is able to cognize the depth and vastness of the process that he or she is a part of, that the creative principle can awaken to itself. As we have seen, that principle cannot know itself directly through a stone, a worm, a butterfly, a giraffe. Even the majority of human beings are not cognizant of the evolutionary impulse in this way. Those who have to struggle from day to day just to survive and feed their families don't have the luxury of the time or education to even begin to think about these philosophical questions. But those of us at the very leading edge of cultural development today are in a different position altogether. That's why I often say we are the luckiest people that have ever been born in the history of our species.

Think about it for a moment: if you are reading a book like this, the likelihood is that you are among the luckiest people who have ever been born. To begin with, you are one of those privileged to have received a high degree of education. People like you and me have access to information that wasn't available until very recently—about the life process, about our psychological interiors, our biological functioning, our cultural development, the natural history of our planet, and the evolution of the expanding cosmos. Besides this wealth of knowledge, we also have a degree of material wealth, comfort, security, and leisure time that is historically unprecedented. The standard of living that we take for granted, kings and queens of old could not have imagined. And on top of all this, we enjoy a degree of freedom that is unparalleled—personal, political, religious, and philosophical. There have never been human beings who have had the extraordinary liberty we have to experiment with our own lives—to *think* in whatever way we want, to *do* almost anything we want, to *say* anything we want, to *go* anywhere we want, to *be* whatever we want.

If you let this in, you will marvel at how lucky you really are, how blessed, how fortunate. The problem is, most of us don't seem to know it. We don't act as if it is true. *The luckiest people in the world don't seem to be aware of how lucky they are.* The significant minority of us who do have the time, the circumstances, and the level of development to be able to be conscious vehicles for the evolutionary impulse are too busy worrying about ourselves. The tragic irony of our cultural predicament is that many of the most highly evolved and privileged people on the planet are lost in an emotional, psychological, philosophical, and spiritual relationship to life that tends to be very superficial.

Do you live as if you knew that you were potentially the leading edge of the interior of the evolving cosmos? Do you act as if the energy and intelligence that initiated the creative process was depending on the choices that you make and the actions that you take? The lives that so many of us lead are clearly disconnected from this overwhelming truth. Most of us appear to be oblivious to our extraordinary good fortune. Even if we're intellectually capable of recognizing it, we still don't tend to *feel* very lucky. More often than not, we feel miserable, victimized, sorry for ourselves. Most of us are so absorbed in our small personal worlds that we hardly even glimpse the big picture. From a vast, cosmic perspective, it's a tragedy. It's a waste of evolution's gifts. Too many of us are simply not available for these higher potentials to emerge within us, because our attention is so distracted. God could be shouting, "I need you!" at the top of His or Her lungs, and we wouldn't even hear.

This state of affairs is what I often call "the postmodern predicament." And it's not *your* predicament—it's *our* predicament. It's not a personal problem; it's a cultural, cosmic, and evolutionary problem. To grasp the picture I'm trying to share, you need to make the effort to look at it not from your ego's perspective but from the perspective of the process itself.

In order to do this, let's once again entertain a theological fantasy. Imagine, for a moment, that you are God—the energy and intelligence that initiated the creative process. And as that divine creator, you are utterly dependent upon human beings to be able to know who you are and consciously act in the cosmos that you have created. You have gradually nurtured, over billions of years of biological evolution, the emergence of ever-more complex forms of life. You have cultivated, over tens of thousands of years of cultural evolution, the human capacity for higher consciousness and cognition. Finally, a moment came where human beings could recognize you directly—not as animistic nature spirits, embodied superheroes, or an anthropomorphic father figure in the sky. In the past few thousand years, following in the footsteps of the greatest mystics from the emerging religious traditions, they began to awaken to your infinite nature in the depths of consciousness, as the timeless, formless ground of Being. And now, in the past few hundred years, they are starting to be able to recognize that you are also that dynamic force which is driving evolutionary Becoming throughout the cosmos.

Because they now have the ability to know you directly as both Being *and* Becoming, you can, at long last, consciously enter into the process through their human hearts and minds. But then, as God, you look at these precious vehicles that you have patiently created for no other purpose than your own conscious participation in the process, and what are they doing? They are lost in their separate, privileged, personal worlds, with little or no sense of who they really are, oblivious to the grandeur and the majesty of what it could mean to live your glory as themselves. As long as they're trapped in their personal worlds, they are of little use to you—you can't take your own next step through them. So your creative powers would be inhibited in the realm of manifestation by their unknowing self-absorption. You would be forced to wait, in divine frustration, for the luckiest people who have ever been born to awaken.

IT MAY BE A BIG STRETCH to see your own life from this God's-eye view, from the vantage point of the creative principle. But if you are serious about the evolution of the interior of the cosmos, it's essential that you do. Unless you are able to see your own presence here within its ever-evolving cosmic and cultural context, it will be difficult to have spiritual confidence, to know what the most appropriate next steps are. The teaching of Evolutionary Enlightenment is about the evolution of cosmos and culture *as yourself.* So it is essential that you make the effort to see your own self and your life-circumstances from the biggest possible perspective, and relate to your own predicament as our shared predicament.

The particular cultural predicament that the luckiest people to have ever been born find themselves in is ironic and paradoxical. The greatest achievement that the creative process has produced in us, the miraculous capacity that makes it possible for consciousness and culture to evolve through us, has become our prison and the biggest obstacle to our higher development. I'm speaking about our uniquely postmodern, highly individuated separate self-sense.

The individuated self is one way that ego is often defined. And in this sense of the word, I like to say that the ego is both your best friend and your worst enemy. It is your best friend because, in the most positive sense, it represents your capacity to individuate—to see yourself as a unique, autonomous entity and to bear witness to your own experience with some measure of objectivity. Individuation is what makes it possible for you to be a conscious agent of evolution, a vessel for Spirit in action. The more profound our individuation, the more powerfully Spirit can shine through us. However, ego is also our worst enemy. For too many of us, as I have described, over-identification with our separate individuality obscures the deeper and higher spiritual dimensions of our being.

The more the self evolves, the more individuated we become, the more our ego develops, in the positive sense, the greater our capacity is to see our experience of consciousness *in context*. When you're a small baby, almost all you are aware of is your biological impulses; there is little if any ability to distinguish between yourself and the world around you. As you develop and mature, you gain a greater capacity to differentiate between your internal experience and your external environment, enabling you to more clearly define yourself as a separate and distinct entity. In this process, you are able to see your life in greater and more inclusive contexts, which means that as you individuate, you also consciously embrace more and more of the universe, both internal and external. In this way, through you, the energy and intelligence that created the universe is able to not only see more and more of its own creation, but engage consciously with it, in all its ever-increasing complexity. The ego, in this sense, is the greatest achievement that the creative process has produced. That's why I say it's our best friend.

It is also, however, our worst enemy, because today many of us have, as I have been describing, become so over-identified with our individual self-sense and its personal story that in spite of being able to cognize more of the cosmos than any human beings have ever been able to, we have lost touch with our deeper spiritual purpose within that cosmos. Because many of us have grown up in a modern and postmodern secular context that recognizes no higher universal truth beyond the fears and desires, whims and preferences of the personal self, slowly but surely the ego has become our most cherished reference point. We have allowed it to usurp the central place that God or Spirit used to hold in traditional cultures.

In traditional cultures, God or Spirit was the unquestioned reference point for higher meaning and purpose. But those of us at the leading edge of modern and postmodern culture today have largely rejected what we perceived as outdated traditional moral, philosophical, and spiritual worldviews. And as of yet, we haven't really found anything to replace them as a source of higher meaning and purpose. That is why, at this moment in history, for the most privileged people in the world, the ego has become so focused on itself.

Evolution's great achievement—our capacity for individuation—has in many ways become a dead end. When you have a highly developed ego without a spiritual context and a deeper sense of purpose, it's likely to be an unhealthy situation. In the way that I perceive it, there is just too much evolutionary potential in the individuated self for its only reference point to be a small personal "I." Remember, from the perspective of evolution, the emergence of the individuated self is quite a triumph. But in our culture, there is no clear upward channel through which that self's greater potential can be realized, and therefore, it inevitably turns in on itself, creating a distortion in the personality and in the culture we build together.

There is no psychological solution to these problems. The only solution is spiritual. The solution is discovering the ego is not the center of the universe; it's but a small part of a very big picture. When you discover that who you truly are is the God-impulse, you see that your ego is just a psychological structure, a highly sophisticated vehicle through which the energy and intelligence that initiated the evolutionary process can more consciously and deliberately engage with the world. Surely, it was never intended to be merely a vehicle for self-absorption and self-infatuation.

At the beginning of the twenty-first century, for the luckiest people who have ever been born, it seems that our passionate pursuit of individuation has reached its apex. We have discovered that we are part of a vast, complex, multidimensional fourteen-billion-year process that is evolving, right now, *as ourselves*. And our ability to recognize this vast trajectory that lies behind us and that still lives within us allows us to appreciate the tremendous significance of the moment we are in, as we reach for the next stage of cultural and cosmic emergence.

The awakening to this evolutionary perspective shatters the postmodern predicament. And it is up to those of us who recognize this liberating context—the luckiest people in the world—to make ourselves available to the energy and intelligence that has, over tens of thousands of years, patiently cultivated our human capacity for higher consciousness and cognition, so that it can take the next step, through us and *as us*.

# CHAPTER 10

# A Moral Imperative

WHEN YOU BEGIN TO AWAKEN to a perspective beyond postmodern individualism, in which you see your own human experience in the context of an evolving culture and cosmos, it changes everything. When you appreciate that it has taken the universe almost fourteen billion years to make it possible for you to have the experience that you are having right now, the way you see the world around you is affected dramatically. When you discover dimensions of your own self and of life itself that are infinitely deeper and higher than your culturally conditioned individuated self-sense, that "personal" dimension of your experience is now seen as an important but small part of a very big picture. In this shift of perspective, the way you understand and approach the spiritual path changes.

For far too many of us modern and postmodern men and women, embarking on a spiritual path has become just another chapter in the ongoing drama of our personal development. From a certain point of view, this could be seen as another expression of our cultural tendency toward narcissism—a spirituality that is focused too much upon our own hopes and fears, triumphs and failures. But it's not our fault that we tend to see it this way. From the moment we came into this world, many of us have been taught to believe that life is all about *me*. Think about it: Did your parents or teachers ever tell you that you were a very small part of a vast evolutionary continuum? Indeed, did they encourage you to feel responsible for the future of that process, to see your every choice and action in a nothing-less-than-cosmic context? Did you grow up with a sense of moral obligation to make our world a better place, or even more audaciously, to be the one to take the next evolutionary step for us all? If not, then it is entirely understandable that, like so many of us, you have become accustomed to relating to the world primarily through the lens of your own personal needs, desires, hopes, and dreams. It makes sense that even your spiritual aspirations are seen as a fundamentally personal matter. That's simply what we've been taught—that's the worldview our individualistic culture has created within us.

When you awaken to the truth that your human experience of consciousness and cognition, your personal presence here on this small planet, is part of an infinitely bigger process than you had ever imagined, you may notice an uncomfortable and perhaps unfamiliar sensation stirring within you—a sense of *obligation*.

In earlier eras in our history, we were accustomed to feeling obligated—to our tribes, to our religious traditions, and in more recent times, to our nations. But in the past few decades, as I have explained, many of us at the leading edge of cultural development have become more identified with being a unique individual than with anything else. Growing up in the secular postmodern world, we have no higher spiritual context that we feel obliged to uphold. As a result, unknowingly, we tend to lack a moral center. In a culture that values individual freedoms above and beyond anything else, it is all too easy to become self-centered and narcissistic. But when we discover that our highly evolved capacity for individuality is not separate from an ever-complexifying deep-time cosmic continuum, this engenders a profound sense of connectedness with the entire evolutionary process.

As our awareness expands dramatically in the direct realization of the nonduality of absolute interrelatedness, our small, personal bubble of separate individuality bursts. Slowly but surely, we awaken to a powerfully implicating new moral context for our existence. This new context is based upon the enlightening recognition that who and what we are—from the matter that makes up the structures of our physical bodies to our miraculous capacity for deep interiority, consciousness, and self-reflection—is all part and parcel of an evolving cosmic process.

MORAL AWARENESS, OR HIGHER CONSCIENCE, is not a static or fixed capacity in the human experience. Like every aspect of who and what we are, it has emerged as part of a deep-time developmental process, and has been evolving for tens of thousands of years, as culture has evolved. The level of our moral development is indicated by how much of the cosmos we are capable of including in our hearts and minds.

For example, at the dawn of human civilization, when we lived in tribes, it was difficult to experience a sense of connection or moral bond with any other human beings who did not share our bloodlines. These exclusive "ethnocentric" moral boundaries still exist today in groups and cultures all over the world. A few thousand years ago, with the birth of the world's great wisdom traditions, our moral capacity took a big leap forward, and included all those who shared our mythic beliefs and religious convictions. With the advent of the modern era, and the birth of the nation state, a different expression of moral inclusion emerged, which now embraced all those who were fellow citizens of our own country. The most recent great leap forward in our evolving capacity for moral inclusion is the emergence of what is called "worldcentric" awareness. In this leading-edge capacity for consciousness, many of us are now able to see ourselves first and foremost as citizens of Planet Earth. The sphere of our moral awareness now embraces the entire globe and all of its many inhabitants.

But there is one more step in this expansion of our capacity for moral inclusiveness. And this is what is called a "cosmocentric" perspective. This barely emergent big-picture moral sensibility arises when we discover and awaken to the deep-time evolutionary context that we have been exploring throughout these pages.

WHEN WE AWAKEN TO A cosmocentric stage of moral awareness, we can no longer simply look at ourselves and our actions from an individual or personal perspective. Nor can we consider our impact only in relation to our tribe, our nation, or even our planet. Now, we begin to see literally everything we are and everything we do in the context of the evolutionary process itself.

What does this mean? Consider this for a moment: if you or I, as highly conscious beings are, as far as we know, at the leading edge of the entire evolutionary unfolding that started with the big bang, then from a certain point of view, what we do is a reflection of the process as a whole. In other words, the way in which you engage with the world around you is a *statement* that reveals how you see and understand the process that gave life to you. The way you express your own humanity—your greater or lesser degree of inspired virtue, moral sensitivity, and spiritual awareness—is a demonstration of what the leading edge of the process actually looks like. Your life—the life you are living right now—is always an evolutionary event, a public statement that says something significant about life itself. The way you are, as an individual, from one moment to another, is your personal contribution to what cosmic evolution looks like here and now, in human form.

If we aspire to live a spiritual life—a life that exemplifies the most deeply positive human virtues—and to some degree we succeed, then we are making a positive statement about how far we have come in our shared evolutionary journey. But if we choose—consciously or unconsciously—to live a life of mediocrity, then we are also making a statement. Because we are not flourishing, what we are saying, whether we intend to or not, is that the evolutionary process is not flourishing.

⊡

IMAGINE THAT THERE WAS a highly evolved intelligent life-form from another dimension, another universe, another planet, looking through a powerful telescope into this dimension, into this universe. And out of all the stars in our galaxy, that intelligent life form decided to focus on our little planet. He, she, or it wanted to know—what was life on Earth all about? And for some reason that telescope ended up pointing at you. Suddenly, you became the representative of all of us. And that extraterrestrial observer closely followed all of your choices and your actions. What would that highly evolved being conclude about the nature of life on our small planet? Would he, she, or it be inspired to come here? It would completely depend on you. It's a funny thought that points to a serious truth. Each and every one of us really is a representative of the entire evolutionary process and how far it has come.

When life is lived in a merely personal context, your choices don't *seem* to matter that much, beyond how you and perhaps those closest to you may feel about them. Whether you succeed or fail, whether you are happy or miserable, it's ultimately your private affair. But in an awakened evolutionary context, your life is no longer private. Once again, your individual life is a statement about life itself, about the nature and meaning of the entire process. And if we look at this through a theological lens, and understand God to be the energy and intelligence driving the process, then we could say that your life is a statement about the nature of God.

Think about that for a moment—it's quite profound. Your life is a statement about who and what God is and how far that absolute principle has evolved. In most traditional mythic religious contexts, where God or Spirit is seen as something "up there," separate from the human world, it is possible to believe in an ultimate source of meaning, goodness, and moral virtue that is not necessarily dependent on our choices and actions. But in our newly emerging cosmocentric context, where we are just awakening to the fact that God or Spirit *is* the evolutionary impulse, and that impulse is animating our very own *self*, then it becomes up to us alone, as evolving, conscious beings, to be the living expression of what we recognize God or Spirit to be *in action*. It is this recognition that gives rise to a new and culturally relevant kind of moral sensibility in the human heart and mind.

As we begin to awaken to a cosmocentric orientation, it's important to come to terms with a hard truth about the life-process: *the evolutionary impulse is not, in and of itself, inherently moral.* That impulse, which is the energy and intelligence driving the entire process, is a wild and impersonal force of nature. It is only as that impulse moves through the developing emotional, psychological, cultural and spiritual structures of the human heart and mind that it awakens and gradually gains the power to reflect upon itself and to express itself with the moral sensitivity that is part of the unique human contribution to the evolving cosmic process. This may be a subtle point, but its implications are profound.

It's easier to understand this when you think about that same energy and intelligence as it is expressed on a physical level, as sexual energy. The procreative impulse has only one purpose: the propagation of the species. That energy is not an individual, and in and of itself it doesn't really care about individuals. As individuals, we *experience* the movement of that impersonal force of nature, and how we choose to respond to it and express it depends on our own level of development, including our cultural values, our moral capacity, our spiritual sensitivity, and so on.

Consider for a moment the difference between when sexual energy moves through an individual with little or no moral sensitivity or self-control and when it moves through a highly developed, morally evolved human being. The different way these individuals respond to the same untamed nature of the biological imperative reflects how our moral development directly influences the way that energy is expressed and how it enters into the world. It works the same way when that impulse emerges at a higher level, as the spiritually inspired urge to evolve at the level of consciousness.

Just as the sexual impulse is only concerned with insuring that the human species doesn't die out, the evolutionary impulse is only interested in creating the future *now*. We could say that its nature is love, but it is an impersonal, wild, fierce, unyielding love that cares only about the evolution of the process, and not necessarily about the personal circumstances of any particular individual. The emergence of that spiritual impulse in our own consciousness is a very profound event, but without being supported by our own higher development, its expression will inevitably lack a moral grounding.

Remember, without higher moral development, without a deeply evolved soul, even spiritual impulses can go awry. The level of development and refinement of that human soul through which that energy enters this world always modifies and affects to a large degree its expression and transmission. So for that impersonal creative energy, that God-force, to express and manifest itself in this world with ever-greater sensitivity, moral inclusiveness, and subtlety of discrimination, our own soul—which I define as our capacity for ever-greater moral being—must be cultivated and developed.

As THE POWERFUL ENERGY AND INTELLIGENCE that initiated the creative process gradually awakens to itself in the light of our highly evolved, self-reflective awareness—especially in the awareness of those who are at the most advanced stage of their culture's development—*evolution begins to happen not only in the individuals but in consciousness itself.* The growing complexity of the self-structure at this level of development acts as a dynamic catalyst that compels consciousness to evolve as it moves through the self into this world. That's why, when the evolutionary impulse awakens and surges through you, your level of moral and spiritual development—the state of your soul—is so critical. The degree to which you have cultivated your best human qualities will determine how much the creative process is able to evolve and to refine itself as it moves through you. When you experience a higher state of consciousness, no doubt it profoundly affects you. But have you ever considered how *you* affect *it? That's* why our development matters so much! That's why our enlightenment is so essential. That is where our spiritual evolution becomes a moral imperative.

In Evolutionary Enlightenment, the individual must come to terms with the profoundly implicating recognition that as we evolve, the process that created us also evolves. In the new evolutionary spirituality, the whole point is that we are all part of one nondual unfolding. When you have seen this for yourself, it becomes a source of tremendous spiritual strength, moral courage, and clarity of purpose. It empowers you at a soul level and spiritualizes the human experience in the deepest way possible. As you awaken to the wild and impersonal nature of the evolutionary impulse, as your Authentic Self, you recognize more and more deeply that it is literally up to *you* to refine that God-energy through the spiritual development of your own soul. That is the most profound realization: that your own development *is* the evolution of God in manifest form. In the end, spiritual development is not *your* development: it is the evolution of God through you.

**PART III**

# The Path and the Goal

# INTRODUCTION TO PART III

As we move into Part III of this book, we are making the transition from theory to practice. As we do so, it is important to understand a subtle and profound truth that some of the greatest spiritual masters and teachers throughout history have told us: *the path and the goal are one.*

The goal is the spontaneous arising of spiritual freedom. In the context of Evolutionary Enlightenment, this essentially means that the fundamental obstacles to one's own capacity to participate whole-heartedly in the life process have been transcended. As a result, one is free to fly on the wings of the Authentic Self, becoming a powerful expression of the evolutionary impulse in human form.

The path is the means by which, through noble effort, one reaches that goal. But always remember, the path and the goal are one. The very desire to embark on a spiritual path and to engage in spiritual practice *is already* the dawning of spiritual freedom, because that desire is the felt vibration and pulsation of the Authentic Self striving to awaken within us.

*The path and the goal are one* means that the *experience* of freedom and the *practice* of freedom are one and the same. The desire to be free that inspires us to practice is never separate from the goal of liberation that we are reaching for. By acting, here and now, on that profound aspiration, we manifest the immediacy of our own potential for liberation.

Once again, the fruition of the path of Evolutionary Enlightenment is realized in the profound awakening of the Authentic Self. The *practice* of Evolutionary Enlightenment has two fundamental components that reflect the two domains of Being and Becoming. In the domain of Being, the practice is learning to master the timeless art and science of meditative stillness. In the domain of evolutionary Becoming, the practice is defined by Five Fundamental Tenets—*Clarity of Intention, The Power of Volition, Face Everything and Avoid Nothing, The Process Perspective, and Cosmic Conscience.* For those who aspire to walk this path in earnest, these tenets must be lived at all times, in all places, under all circumstances.

If the egoless passion of the Authentic Self has not yet become your natural and spontaneous state, you will find that through embracing the art and science of stillness, and making the noble effort to put the Five Tenets into practice, your personality will nevertheless become an expression of that very same spiritual freedom, here and now. The path and the goal are one.

**CHAPTER 11**

# The Art and Science of Stillness

THE PATH OF EVOLUTIONARY ENLIGHTENMENT, like all enlightenment teachings, is a path of ego-transcendence. In Evolutionary Enlightenment, however, transcending ego is not an end in itself—it's a means to a higher end. The reason that we want to have the liberating experience of transcending our personal fears and desires and our culturally conditioned values is first and foremost to open up some *space* within the self—space for evolution to occur.

Why is this important? Because being inspired by the idea of conscious evolution is one thing, while actually engaging in the process of evolution is something else altogether. Many people are moved by the notion of evolutionary becoming. But within themselves they are not free. They are trapped in psychological hang-ups and attachments, with little or no space for that which is new. Their souls are not liberated, and their choices and actions are still being shaped by unconscious adherence to values and perspectives that have nothing to do with being a liberated vessel for the evolution of consciousness and culture. Merely being inspired by the potential for conscious evolution does not automatically give us access to the fearless inner freedom to actualize that potential. In order to find that freedom, to open up that space for the new, it is essential that you liberate yourself to a significant degree from your personal fears and desires and your culturally conditioned values.

The inner freedom I am describing is not different from the goal of traditional enlightenment. In the traditional approach, however, that freedom is an end in itself. In Evolutionary Enlightenment, as I have explained, the attainment of spiritual freedom is not the end of the path but, ideally, becomes the foundation from which to engage in conscious evolution. So the foundation of the path and practice of Evolutionary Enlightenment is nothing less than the position of traditional enlightenment itself. In order to release your own consciousness and psyche for the wider and deeper embrace of the life process that Evolutionary Enlightenment demands, you must disentangle yourself, you must significantly free yourself from your karma, your history, your culture, and your personal ego.

How does one discover enlightened awareness? There are two ways that you can gain access to the intoxicating joy and ecstatic wakefulness of that timeless spiritual attainment: spontaneously, or through making noble effort.

Like an unexpected visit from God, for no particular reason, the doors of perception can spontaneously open, expanding your awareness to reveal a higher and deeper dimension of your own consciousness. This kind of spontaneous experience often happens in the company of a spiritual master who has access to this unmanifest ground, or among a group of inspired individuals who have come together to share mystical truths.

You can also, however, assume the posture of freedom and experience enlightened awareness simply through disciplined effort. Traditionally, the metaphor for this radical freedom has been the image of the seated Buddha, perfectly still, eyes closed, his awareness focused within, his attention on the infinite nature of his own consciousness.

So the way to practice this radical position is to literally take the posture he is taking—to engage with what I call "the art and science of stillness" or the traditional practice of meditation.

The ability to be very still is foundational, because stillness is the perennial portal that gives us access to the dimension of ourselves and of life itself that is the source of traditional enlightenment. In learning how to be still, you are choosing to stand for and express that deepest part of yourself—that empty no-place before the beginning of time, before anything ever happened. That formless ground of Being is always the deepest dimension of who we all are, and it is the ultimate source and wellspring of all that is. In that ground, nothing ever moves, because there is no time, no form, no subject or object. There is only One, eternally at rest and at peace. By assuming the inner and outer position of stillness, you are bearing witness to the deepest part of yourself in the world of time and space.

It is important to put a lot of time into practicing the art and science of stillness, until you become firmly rooted in the enlightened position it represents. Meditation is very simple. It is a *posture*—not as much a physical posture as an inner posture in relationship to your experience. Outwardly, it is important to be able to sit still and be deeply at ease and alert. Inwardly, being still means having no relationship whatsoever to anything that is happening, has happened, or will ever happen. *Be still, relax, pay attention, and assume no relationship to anything that arises.* That is the posture of freedom.

RIGHTLY UNDERSTOOD, MEDITATION AND ENLIGHTENMENT are one and the same. Meditation is the experience of a particular state of consciousness that has certain qualities, which are also the qualities of enlightened awareness. This is why meditation can be understood as a *metaphor* for enlightenment. When you meditate, you consciously choose to assume the enlightened relationship to your own experience, which means you are *letting everything go*.

I'm pointing to an *inner* position in relationship with your own mind and emotions—a position that is free from compulsive identification with fear and desire, with time, thought, memory, and feeling. Taking this position requires enormous spiritual courage. If you do it, however, you will discover why the Buddha looks so happy and so peaceful. You will experience the joy of letting everything go—all the thoughts, feelings, and sensations that arise.

When you look at a powerful statue of the Buddha, you can see, in his face and posture, his experience of the *freedom from* the momentum of karma and from all the fears and desires that are associated with it. That peace is attractive for any of us who are tormented by the movement of our own minds, and by the unpredictable rollercoaster of our emotional experience. It promises release from the frustration of ongoing existential confusion, repeated disappointments, and endless craving after things that are ultimately insubstantial. If you have the courage to let go of everything, while practicing the art and science of stillness, you will get a sense, or an intimation, of what the Buddha's experience might have been like. But you have to authentically do it. Imagine what it would be like to let go of everything and to have no desire for anything other than utter and unconditional release.

In order to experience this inner freedom, when you sit down to meditate, you should be holding on to nothing. The whole point is to have no attachment whatsoever—no attachment to life, no attachment to death, no attachment to anything in this world. It is not a matter of letting go of any *thing* in particular. If there is something specific that's troubling you psychologically and emotionally, you can try to let go of it and you may feel more peaceful, but that's not meditation—and it's not freedom. Many people think that if they could just let go of this or that, they would be free. But if you are going to be free in a context of enlightenment, you have to be willing to let go of *everything*. The freedom of enlightenment itself is only won through letting go absolutely. So in the posture of meditation, which is a metaphor for enlightenment itself, unless in every moment you are letting go of everything, you are wasting your time.

Meditation only becomes real, powerful, authentic, and *liberating* when it is a practice of letting everything go. Otherwise it is reduced to little more than a psycho-spiritual relaxation technique. It may make you feel better, but it won't set you free. Feeling better and being free don't necessarily mean the same thing. Feeling better is relative; being free is not. Ultimately, spiritual freedom depends on how profound is your ability to let go of everything—and not just once, but over and over again. If you understand what it means to let go of everything, you know everything you need to know about meditation. Then your meditation is *real*. It's the posture of freedom, the posture of enlightenment. It's a profound existential stand you are taking in relationship to life and death; a spiritual position you are assuming in relationship to eternity.

So when I teach the art and science of stillness, I embrace the traditional enlightenment as foundational. Meditation, as a metaphor for enlightenment, is the practice of the unconditional willingness to be free from, to transcend, and to let go of anything that is in your way.

THE ALL-IMPORTANT REASON we need to take this position, once again, is that most of us are simply not available for the enormous task of conscious evolution. We are too busy with the contents of our own mind, hypnotized by the fears and desires of our personal egos, and paralyzed by the beliefs and expectations of culture. Our thoughts and emotions are like an ongoing drama that holds our attention captive. How available can we be for the creative process when our attention is distracted, when the self is still caught in a psychological prison and limited by unenlightened cultural perspectives?

If you feel trapped by what's happening within your own mind, you are also inevitably going to feel trapped by what's happening in the world around you. The relationship that you have with *life* always starts with the relationship you have with your own mind and emotions. Unknowingly, we tend to build prisons in our minds and then we live in them. This is why we need to be very careful about which particular thoughts and feelings we choose to identify with and, even more importantly, to act upon. The thoughts or emotions that you choose to follow have karmic consequences. Once you act upon a thought or an emotion, a whole chain of events is set in motion—a lifetime can be built on a single thought. Too much of the time, we are barely conscious of which thoughts or feelings we are choosing to follow, and why: Are we blindly reacting to the prejudices and predispositions of the culturally conditioned self? Are we continually swayed by the fears and desires of our personal ego? Or are we fearlessly responding to our higher and deeper impulses, to the call of our own Authentic Self? The relationship that you have with thought, with the content of consciousness, will determine your destiny.

THE REASON YOU MEDITATE is not to *become* free. When you awaken to the ground of Being, you discover that you *already are* free. In this deepest part of your self, nothing has ever happened. You have not been born; even time itself has not yet begun. The purpose of meditation is to recognize, over and over and over again, that you are already free. If your practice has power, if your experience of the ground of Being is deep and profound, you will discover and redis-cover that, in truth, you are not a prisoner. You are not held captive by your own mind, nor are you imprisoned by your thoughts and emotions. This timeless mystical insight sounds so simple, but it's so, so easy to forget.

The ground of Being is a deeper, infinitely more subtle dimension of your own consciousness that cannot be perceived by the gross fac-ulties of the conditioned mind and ego. You can't see the ground of Being; you can't taste it; you can't touch it. Even if you have directly experienced the unconditioned freedom of that empty ground, when you return to the world of conditioned mind and ego, you're likely to doubt it. *The mind simply cannot cognize this dimension of formless Being, and the ego cannot know it.* That's why it's important to practice the art and science of stillness as much as you can. If you meditate regularly, with a strong intention, you will keep rediscovering that you are not a prisoner. You cannot recognize that enough. Until your conviction in your own freedom is unwavering, and you're able to prove it through unbroken consistency in the way that you live, meditate every day as if your life depended on it. You *need* to keep having that experi-ence. Each and every time you realize that you're not a prisoner, it gives you a deeper confidence in that empty ground that is your own deepest self. It builds a conscious conviction in the liberating truth of no-limitation.

When you practice the art and science of stillness, you must strive to maintain that *posture* of unconditional freedom, *no matter what your inner experience may be.* In that posture, you disengage your attention from attachment to and identification with all thoughts, images, memories, emotions, beliefs, and convictions, and simply allow it to come to rest upon awareness itself. If you want to be a liberated vessel for the evolutionary impulse, you must learn how to directly experience the chaos and confusion of your own mind without being disturbed by any of it. *Only if you can bear it will you be able to take responsibility for it.* If *you* can't calmly endure the chaos of your own mind, others will inevitably suffer the consequences. If you can't handle the movement of your own thoughts and emotions with ease, while you are simply being still and paying attention, then how are you ever going to make the appropriate choices when you are walking, talking, and engaging with others? *Meditation is training for life. Stillness is training for action.*

When you assume no relationship to the content of consciousness, it doesn't matter what arises—you may experience the most sublime, ecstatic, and liberating revelations; you may be swamped by mundane and meaningless chatter; or you may be overwhelmed by frightening and irrational thoughts and impulses. But you remain disengaged and unmoved. Once again, we all have to be careful with the choices we make in relationship to our own internal experience, day to day, hour to hour, moment to moment, because there are *always* consequences. Whenever you allow yourself to be thrown around unconsciously by the inner storms of thought and emotion, and even worse, make wrong choices as a result, you will always pay a price for it. The worst part of that price is your own confidence, and your own belief in your capacity to evolve. But if, like the Buddha, you remain motionless and radically disengaged, inwardly and outwardly, when the storm passes, you'll experience a tremendous sense of exhilaration. You will realize that your own heart's conviction is more powerful than the chaos of your mind.

That being said, it is no easy task to disembed our consciousness from a habitual and conditioned identification with thought and emotion. In order to discover what an appropriate, conscious, freely chosen relationship to our own experience could be, the first step, once again, is always to have no relationship to any of it.

To go beyond the mind, you have to first reject the mind completely. Discovering what it means to stand free from the whole conditioned flow of thought is absolutely fundamental. It's prior to anything else. *Our relationship to thought is everything.* It's what determines how free we will be to create our own destiny and to consciously participate in the evolutionary process. Learning what it means to assume no relationship to the content of consciousness is the critical step in making it possible for you to align yourself with the Authentic Self, rather than the ego. Taking this bold step will enable you to take control of your own life in a way that nothing else can.

Letting go of everything certainly doesn't mean we should conclude that all the contents of the mind and memory are wrong. Much of our history is of great value, and the highly developed capacities for emotion and cognition are some of evolution's greatest gifts to us. But if we want to be free, we have to be willing to let go of all of it *first* and then see how it looks *after* the fact. Only through letting go of everything will we eventually come to rest in the infinite ground of Being. That is the place from which we can make miracles happen. That kind of unconditional freedom is the foundation that makes conscious evolution possible.

As I said in the opening pages of this chapter, on the path of Evolutionary Enlightenment, the posture of stillness is not an end in itself. For those of us who are committed to the evolution of consciousness and culture, and who are endeavoring to participate wholeheartedly in the life process, we cannot *remain* in that posture of no relationship. Quite the opposite. To be an evolutionarily enlightened human being, you must cultivate dynamic and deeply creative relationships with time, with thought, with feeling, with others, with the world. And those relationships must be constantly informed by conscious, *liberated* attention, rather than by the unconscious conditioned assumptions of the personal and cultural ego.

Your attention will become liberated by learning to assume the enlightened posture of no relationship. In this way, you can discover over and over and over again what it means to have a completely *fresh*, ever-new beginning to your relationship with time, thought, feeling, others, and the world. The experience of enlightened awareness is the perpetual knowing of that place within yourself where there is always an ever-new beginning. It's the ongoing revelation that anything is possible. That is what we discovered when we traveled all the way back to before the beginning of time—that in that mysterious no-place *nothing has ever happened ... and that is why everything is possible.*

If the mysterious knowing that everything is possible becomes your fundamental and consistent reference point, then you will be an evolutionarily enlightened human being. You will always have access, in some way, shape, or form, to a perspective in which nothing has ever happened and everything is always possible. That's a very different orientation to life than most people can imagine. Too often, our relationship to life is based on conscious and unconscious cynicism and doubt—an underlying presumption of limitation that clouds our perspective on just about everything.

It's important to understand that the experience of this ever-new beginning does not automatically wipe away your past. When you rise from your stillness, you still have to deal with the often harsh realities of human life and the challenges of your own karmic predicament. Your past will still be there, but it will no longer be an overwhelming obstacle to your own higher development. The unavoidable trials of a deeply committed life will continue to confront you, but now, because of where you are rooted, you are always in touch with the immediacy of infinite potential.

In this way, in Evolutionary Enlightenment, the perennial practice of assuming no relationship to the content of consciousness not only aligns you with the inherent freedom of the empty ground of Being, but, even more importantly, it makes space within you for the limitless creative potential of the evolutionary impulse to reveal itself. It forges the emotional conviction that real change is possible, and it generates a renewed faith in your own capacity to evolve.

If you want to develop in profound and significant ways, it is essential that you build up a reservoir of spiritual and emotional conviction, a source of boundless freedom that will give you the energy to transcend the apparent limitations of your own emotional, psychological, and cultural experience. By embracing stillness with deadly seriousness, you cultivate that freedom and conviction in no-limitation as a fundamental existential reference point.

Meditation takes you back to zero, and creates the space for the ever-new beginning that is the essence of enlightened awareness. But always remember that you are the one who has to generate the momentum for your own higher development. Time and time again, you have to let everything go, until there is no question that whatever life confronts you with, you will respond, before thought, from the very best part of yourself—from your own Authentic Self, the evolutionary impulse, that infinite possibility that burst out of nothingness and became the whole universe.

# CHAPTER 12

# Clarity of Intention

THE FIRST TENET OF EVOLUTIONARY ENLIGHTENMENT is called Clarity of Intention. This tenet points directly to the essential nature of the evolutionary impulse itself: the wholehearted, passionate intention to exist, to develop, to become, to *evolve*. That impulse, as we have discovered, is the same uninhibited YES that burst forth as the big bang, that compels the body to procreate and the mind to innovate. When that impulse expresses itself at the highest levels of consciousness, it is experienced as the inspiration that pulls us toward spiritual liberation and enlightenment. It is the mysterious drive to become more conscious. To have Clarity of Intention means to align oneself with the clear and single-pointed purpose of that impulse itself. And the way that alignment occurs, in a human heart and mind, is that *the intention to evolve becomes more important to us than anything else in this world.*

The evolutionary impulse has no other motive than our own individual and collective higher development—perpetual, ecstatic, and uninhibited. It is the vibration of the energy and intelligence that initiated the creative process awakening to itself in you and in me, and its only purpose is to create the future. In that impulse, fear, doubt, hesitation, and obstacles *do not exist.* How could they? Our interest in spiritual evolution doesn't come from the ego. It comes from that mysterious part of yourself and myself that is only interested in becoming more conscious. If you close your eyes and focus upon your own experience of the spiritual impulse as it is moving in you, you will notice that its nature is always overwhelmingly positive. All it ever wants to do is move forward. Ecstatically, it wants to go all the way, holding nothing back, right now.

When you experience that desire to go all the way, you taste a joy and a fearless confidence that doesn't come from the ego. And you know that this alone has the power to take you to the yonder shore.

LIKE EACH OF THE FIVE TENETS, Clarity of Intention is both the path and the goal. It is *already* the nature of your Authentic Self, but it is also a position you can *choose* to take that will get you to the very same place. When engaged with wholeheartedly, this tenet will cultivate within you a liberating confidence in your ability to succeed.

On the path of Evolutionary Enlightenment, Clarity of Intention is empowering, because no matter where you may be at this particular point in your spiritual development, it places the ultimate outcome of the quest directly in your own hands. That outcome always rests on the simple question: *What do I really want—what is more important to me than anything else?*

You may think that you want to evolve, that you want to become spiritually liberated or enlightened. But *how much* do you want it? Is your desire for spiritual evolution more important to you than anything else in this world? Or is it just one of many options among which you pick and choose, according to how you feel on any given day?

Have you ever thought deeply about what really matters most to you? Until you have become clear about your highest intention, it's difficult for any real or consistent development to occur. Many of us have had spiritual experiences in which we momentarily glimpse an indescribable glory—a greater purpose and a higher potential for human life. But too often we are not spiritually mature enough to value those moments of revelation—to value them so highly that we are ready to pay the price to evolve, here and now.

This is understandable—after all, there is very little in our shared cultural background that would prepare us to do so. Because many of us have been deeply conditioned by a worldview characterized by extreme individualism and secular materialism, we have no shared context for honoring and respecting a higher dimension of life that is infinitely greater than the personal sphere. We tend to be culturally unprepared to respond to our own deepest insights, and therefore, even after glimpsing the glory of our spiritual potential, we don't necessarily know how to make the noble effort to transform ourselves for the highest reasons. If you find that after engaging in some form of spiritual practice and even having deep spiritual insights, you still do not change in any significant way, this is probably why.

If you are serious in your desire to evolve, this intention has to become more important to you than anything else in the world. You must learn to value, honor, and respect the highest spiritual potential you have glimpsed in yourself above and beyond all else. Everything comes down to this. Whether or not your spiritual aspiration bears the fruit of radical transformation is entirely dependent upon how much it matters to you. I cannot overstate this. It is the cornerstone of Evolutionary Enlightenment. *Your own Clarity of Intention is everything.*

*What is most important to me?* This seems like a simple question, but its implications are profound. There is no more direct way to shine a light on your own spiritual predicament right now than to sincerely ask yourself: What is most important to me?

Consider this matter very seriously: Based on your own life experience and your own insight into the nature and meaning and purpose of existence, what do you conclude has the greatest value?

Once you have answered this question, then you should ask yourself: *Is the life I am living a clear reflection of that which I have concluded is most important?* Dare to be ruthlessly honest. After all, whatever answer you have come to *should* be the guiding principle of your entire existence. Why? Because you and you alone have decided it has greater value than anything else!

More often than not, thoughtful, spiritually sensitive individuals will admit that their deepest experience of Spirit or God has been more profound, meaningful, and liberating than any other experience in their life. But when they begin to honestly reflect on the principles that are guiding the life they are choosing to live, day to day, they often recognize, in light of those moments of spiritual insight, that there is quite a gap. If this rings true for you, you may need to admit, as many people do, that you don't want to evolve spiritually *more than anything else.* You may long to have those experiences again, to taste the exhilaration of higher states of consciousness. But when any one of us attempts to bridge the gap between those deepest insights and the reality of the way we have chosen to live our own lives, our spiritual predicament is revealed. What we will often find is that we are deeply divided.

In this way, the serious contemplation of the question, *What is most important to me?,* will catalyze a profound confrontation with the actuality of your relationship to life and the different motivations and drives that are operating beneath the surface of your awareness. This contemplation reveals with a piercing clarity the fact that there is one part of you, the Authentic Self, that aspires to evolve, that longs for higher meaning and purpose, for a life of spiritual freedom. But there is also another part, the individual and collective ego, that tends to resist such higher potentials, and holds steadfastly to the way things have been. Once again, in this teaching, "ego" is a shorthand for all the ways in which we are consciously and unconsciously identified with and attached to relative dimensions of self that inhibit our higher spiritual development.

Focusing your attention on your own fundamental intention will allow you to see, maybe for the first time, the dramatic difference between your Authentic Self's unbridled passion for spiritual evolution, and your ego's conditioned hesitation or refusal to let go of the way things have been. It may bring to the surface deep and powerful forces in your own psyche that usually remain hidden. Most importantly, it makes it possible for you to begin to consciously take responsibility for the best part of who you are. It enables you to choose to value that passion for spiritual evolution above and beyond the endless fears, doubts, desires, demands, beliefs, and expectations of your individual and cultural ego.

CLARITY OF INTENTION IS SIMPLE, but its implications are radical, and profound beyond measure. When you know you want to evolve more than anything else, you don't have to depend on the experience of higher states of consciousness; you don't have to wait for God to save you; you don't have to hope for grace to descend. If you remain true to that which matters most, nothing will be able to stop you. The path ahead becomes clear without anyone else needing to show you: you simply put your highest intention first and let everything else come second.

In a truly courageous soul, grappling with this tenet over time will forge a strength and spiritual independence that in and of itself *is* liberation. Clarity of Intention is the foundation of the enlightened life and the key to the evolution of consciousness, because it places your transformation entirely in your own hands. It's a deliberate, freely chosen position. You make choices that take you in the direction that you, in your highest moments, have *decided* to go in, even if, at times, it may not feel comfortable. In fact, how you feel becomes almost irrelevant, because now you have a commitment—a self-created obligation to a higher purpose.

If you are bold enough to aspire to be a vehicle for the evolutionary impulse in this world, commitment must be your foundation. Without that solid ground of unshakable intention, how can you be a stable and trustworthy vessel for the wild and untamed force of nature that is your own Authentic Self? I don't believe it's possible to live a passionate and engaged spiritual life and contribute significantly to the evolution of consciousness and culture without this kind of profound commitment.

In the unenlightened heart and mind, our allegiance lies most often with the fears and desires of the personal ego and the culturally conditioned self. That is why we are often fickle, easily swayed by the ever-changing emotional currents of our personal world and the secular values of our shared culture. Even if we have, on occasion, discovered something higher, enormous effort and patience is usually required to shift that fundamental allegiance. But if you are deadly serious, and you are committed to standing by your own intention to evolve, you will begin to generate an entirely different momentum within yourself. The momentum of your own commitment will enable you to cultivate an emotional connection to a perspective that your ego cannot see or feel or relate to in any way, and that our shared culture does not recognize. And when that emotional connection grows strong, through remaining true to your commitment, you begin to win some degree of authentic spiritual autonomy and independence. You discover soul strength—the spiritually inspired conviction to take responsibility for your own destiny and ultimately, for the destiny of the evolutionary process itself.

THE FUNDAMENTAL COMMITMENT that this tenet calls us to is a moral, philosophical, and spiritual position in relationship to life that each and every one of us has to come to for ourselves. No one can do this for you. What I'm pointing to here is nothing less than the door to your own liberation. Clarity of Intention is truly the foundation of a spiritual life lived in earnest. But it's important to be ready for what sincerely contemplating this tenet may reveal. It can trigger an inner storm of existential confusion, fear, and doubt. Asking a black-and-white question, like "What is more important to me than anything else?," will illuminate your deepest motivations with an unusual degree of clarity. When you seriously consider putting your intention to evolve above all else, you are inadvertently shining a light on all the parts of yourself that don't want anything to do with higher evolution or spiritual freedom. You are, in a sense, calling the dragon out of the cave.

Ego, as I have said, has many faces. Seriously embracing Clarity of Intention reveals an ancient and insidious one, which I often refer to as the *irrational refusal to change*. This manifestation of ego can only really be understood once you have made a commitment to something inconceivably positive and infinitely bigger than the fears and desires of your personal self. The ego seldom unveils this face, except in those rare moments when, having stumbled upon that which is unthinkably sacred and meaningful, you feel compelled to *respond* with all of your being, to declare an unconditional YES to that which you have recognized. Only then will you confront the force of a powerful inertia within, an ever-irrational position that blindly resists, defies, and denies that unbridled positivity. This is when you understand why spiritual masters for millennia have referred to the ego as "the enemy within." That perennial foe is a willful one that abides deep in the human psyche, and always refuses the call from the heart to embrace our highest evolutionary potential.

Most of us go through our entire lives and never see this face of the ego for what it is. And that is because we rarely consider for ourselves what is most important or face the challenge of putting that first, above all else. We tend to avoid the kind of absolute and liberating simplicity that this first tenet points to, preferring to exist in a habitual state of division, ambivalence, and complexity. And under cover of that complexity, the personal and cultural ego can thrive and maintain firm control.

When we aspire to evolve, to live a truly spiritual life, to become an enlightened person, we dare to open our hearts to the thrilling possibility of something so unthinkably glorious that it's just too positive for most of us to bear. This is simply *terrifying* to the ego, because it feels the overwhelming pressure to relinquish control. This is when it emerges out of the shadows and its face can be seen. Only when we dare to even consider saying yes to our highest spiritual aspiration will we become aware of why the ego is, and always has been, the greatest obstacle on the path to enlightenment.

WHEN EMBRACING CLARITY OF INTENTION, consistency is everything. When you first make a heroic commitment to your own evolution, you will experience a surge of liberating confidence, a sense of empowerment, and an often startling conviction in your potential for transformation. But the reason it is so important to cultivate Clarity of Intention is because that conviction probably won't last.

When the ego's irrational refusal is triggered, as sooner or later it will be, you may find yourself lost in a psycho-emotional storm, unable to see one inch in front of you. You may wonder, "How could I experience such unshakable confidence in my own potential for transformation, and then so easily fall into a state of confusion and despair?" But that's the very nature of the divided self. *The ego doesn't want you to become a liberated human being,* and this kind of experience is living proof of that fact. The arising of doubt is the ego's response to your declaration of allegiance to your Authentic Self, to the part of you that wants nothing more than to evolve. The deeper your conviction in your potential to become one with that Authentic Self, the stronger and more violent the ego's recoil will be. Unless you can endure the intensity of this kind of reaction, and stand firm in the face of the temptation to doubt, you are not going to evolve and the higher experiences you have had, no matter how profound, will not amount to lasting transformation.

At such challenging moments, it matters very much that you have *already* come to a decision about what is more important to you than anything else—your own bottom line. That intention becomes your anchor, your buoy in the storm, something you can hold on to no matter how ferociously the ego reacts. If you have already clearly decided what matters most, and made a deep commitment to that above all else, you will find that your own intention is more than enough to hold you steady, even if you temporarily lose touch with all the inspiration and clarity you may have felt before. But if you haven't already resolved this issue, then in those moments of greatest challenge, you will let go of that buoy and find yourself tossed helplessly around on the rocky seas of fear, doubt, and confusion. And you will wake up on the desert island of your own ego, your confidence and faith and commitment weakened, wondering how you could possibly have betrayed your own highest intention.

This is why I always say that consistency is everything. Once you have reached that point in your own spiritual development where you have come to a clear resolution to evolve beyond ego, it is essential to avoid self-betrayal. If you betray that aspiration, which *is* your Authentic Self, you will lose your bearings. And if you betray yourself too many times, you will soon come to a point where you just won't care anymore—slowly but surely you will have lost touch with the passion to actualize your higher potentials. Never forget, we're only human; none of us have infinite strength or spiritual resources, and we must have the humility to respect that fact.

Once you have made a decision to evolve beyond the personal and cultural ego, inspired by the direct experience of your own potential to do so, never doubt that intention. If you have not yet experienced that liberating potential, it makes sense to remain skeptical until it reveals itself within you. Once this has occurred, however, you should not allow yourself to indulge in doubting your own direct experience. For most of us, the liberating state of profound clarity and absolute conviction is not permanent. Such experiences make a deep impact on the soul, inwardly revealing the path to your own evolution and transformation. But that revelation needs to always be protected, so that the path remains open. Clarity of Intention is what enables us to do this. It connects us to a profound source of confidence—a confidence in our own capacity to change and in the transformative power of the evolutionary process.

Any spiritual adventurer who goes through this kind of confrontation with his or her own ego, and comes out the other side without having compromised, will know, directly, a fundamental truth of the evolutionarily enlightened perspective: *the Authentic Self and the ego are two completely different worlds.* You will see for yourself that the perspective the ego creates is never absolutely real in the way you had imagined it to be. In comparison with the spiritually empowered inspiration of the Authentic Self, the ego's petty fears, desires, and concerns are relative and ultimately insubstantial. This is easy to say, but is a hard lesson to learn. When you find yourself under attack, those fears, desires, and concerns won't seem insubstantial or unimportant. They will appear very real indeed.

The dramatic difference between the limited, relative world of the ego and the infinite, absolute nature of the Authentic Self will remain apparent only through the ongoing spiritual practice of contemplating Clarity of Intention. Fueled by the power of your own intention, you can prepare, so that when you find yourself in the midst of what the great realizers call "the dark night of the soul," you will remain cognizant of what matters most and you will doubtlessly hold fast to that and that alone.

WHEN LIVING THE SPIRITUAL LIFE is seen in an evolutionary context, your ability to be true to your own intention is far more than a personal matter. Over time, as your practice and perspective mature, you begin to recognize that there are much greater, *impersonal* consequences to your victory or failure. On the one hand, if you succeed in standing firm in your intention, the interior of the cosmos gains the opportunity to evolve through *you*. On the other hand, if you fail, if you back down, *the creative process itself loses a precious opportunity to evolve*. The evolutionary impulse, or God-principle, loses a vehicle through which to consciously create the future.

From the radically impersonal point of view of the evolution of consciousness, your ultimate value lies in your potential to awaken to the evolutionary impulse as your own Authentic Self, and to consciously take responsibility for the process that *it* initiated. Only when you identify with the Authentic Self and *embrace* the process, will higher as-yet-unmanifest potentials become manifest through you with real power to effect change in this world. *That's* what the process wants. That's why we are each so desperately needed. God, as the creative impulse, or Eros, is interested in you for your higher potentials, for what you are *capable* of; God isn't interested in you as a personal self. You are a potential bearer of the future, and therefore the impulse that is driving the evolutionary process is only interested in you according to how much of that potential you are able to fulfill.

This is the highest context from which to engage with contemplating the first tenet, because it carries with it a sense of overwhelming urgency to come to a resolution about what matters most, here and now and forever. After all, how much time does any one of us need to get over the ego's fears, doubts, and hesitations, and step forward? From a merely personal perspective it will always seem like we have all the time in the world to struggle with our ambivalence and selfishness, to choose to live up to our highest potential or not. But from an impersonal, evolutionary perspective we *never* have more time, because the situation is always urgent. When it comes to those destiny-defining moments in life, if we allow ourselves to put something else above our own intention to evolve, the real loser is God, not us.

As you think about your own spiritual interests in this light, as you contemplate your intention to become an enlightened human being, remember: the energy and intelligence that initiated the creative process is more interested in you than you are in it. The universe is trying to evolve, and it can only evolve *through you*. We are the vehicles through which the manifest God can take the next step. In the end, *your spiritual interest is not about you*. It never was. It's God's interest in Him, Her, or Itself. Those of us who have been culturally conditioned to see the world primarily through a personal lens find that difficult to appreciate, but from a higher cosmocentric perspective, that's simply the way it is. When you become deeply interested in spiritual evolution, the universe becomes even more interested in you. And when you put the intention to evolve above and beyond all else, it's the greatest gift you can give to God—a partner in the evolutionary process emerges in the form of you.

# CHAPTER 13

# The Power of Volition

THE SECOND TENET OF EVOLUTIONARY ENLIGHTENMENT is the Power of Volition. This tenet calls us to a great responsibility. It asks us to endeavor to be responsible for nothing less than the destiny of the evolutionary process, here and now, *as ourselves*. And the way you embrace that Herculean task is through first and foremost making the noble spiritual effort to take responsibility for all of what makes you who you are. That means striving to come to terms with *all* of your past, and all of the karmic consequences of that past. It also means courageously stretching to embrace all the historically accumulated complexity of your present circumstances. Only then will you or I or any one of us be in a spiritually empowered position to consciously create our future.

Why is it so important that we take this enormous responsibility on our own shoulders? *Because it has been ours all along.* But we are only just beginning to awaken to that fact. Remember, when we traveled all the way back to that instant when this entire cosmic process was born, and we located the impulse that caused something to burst out of nothing? We discovered that that evolutionary impulse is the energy and intelligence animating our own Authentic Self. The Power of Volition is about aligning with the profoundly self-implicating recognition that as that primordial impulse, you and you alone are the one who is responsible for all of this—from the initial choice that became the big bang all the way to the brink of the as-yet-uncreated future.

The evolutionary impulse, when it awakens to itself within you as your Authentic Self, has no hesitation whatsoever about embracing that responsibility. How could an energy and intelligence that is powerful and audacious enough to have given rise to an entire universe have issues with responsibility? That surging momentum, which is the force of Eros, the God-impulse, is utterly one-pointed. In that impulse, no fear, no doubt, no hesitation, and no division exist. So when the force of Eros awakens in you, as the Authentic Self, that part of you experiences no ambivalence about being accountable. That part of yourself doesn't *aspire* to be responsible; it already *is*. That is its very nature; it is one with the First Cause itself.

Your ego—both personal and cultural—has many good reasons to resist such an overwhelming responsibility. For many of us, our identity has been shaped, both consciously and unconsciously, by the belief that we are victims—of fate, of circumstances, and of other people. The separate ego does not want to be fully accountable and tends to hide out behind one excuse or another. This attitude is reinforced by the hyper-individualistic postmodern cultural context in which many of us have grown up, a context that tends to foster a sense of victimization. For those of us who have spent a lifetime identifying with the personal ego and the culturally conditioned self, it will require nothing less than a heroic effort and a wholehearted intention to embrace this kind of deeper responsibility for ourselves. Once again, that unhesitating responsibility is *already* the attitude of your Authentic Self, fueled by the energy of the evolutionary impulse. In order to align with that part of yourself, you will need to do whatever it takes to renounce the ego's excuses and proclivity to see itself as a victim.

Until you become aligned with the natural inclination of the Authentic Self, the Power of Volition can be engaged with as a practice that can enable you to get there. Like all of the tenets, this tenet is both the path and the goal. Keep in mind that the practices I teach are never merely techniques. They point directly to what the self-liberated posture of Evolutionary Enlightenment *already* is. They only seem like techniques from the point of view of the unenlightened mind. But in fact, they simply reveal how evolutionarily enlightened awareness looks out upon the world. From that liberated perspective, the expression of the Authentic Self is always wholehearted intention, which is what the first tenet is all about. And it is an attitude of unconditional responsibility, which is what the second tenet points to.

THAT BEING SAID, engaging with the second tenet as a practice is no small matter. It means actively and deliberately endeavoring to take responsibility for your past, your present, and your future.

Taking responsibility for your past means unconditionally accepting the fact that you are here, right now, *because of your own choices.* I don't just mean the decisions you made yesterday, or last week, or even last year. From the biggest cosmocentric perspective, that responsibility reaches all the way back to the beginning of time, through every stage of the evolutionary journey. It started at the very first moment, with the original choice to become, when you, as the primordial creative impulse, made that momentous decision to create something out of nothing. It embraces everything that has happened as a result of that cosmos-creating choice—including but infinitely transcending the personal and cultural experiences that have shaped your personality and your self-sense in this particular lifetime.

Why is it so important to take responsibility for the entirety of your past, for all of your creative and karmic history? In the context of Evolutionary Enlightenment, it's to make you *available*—available to participate in the present and the future in ways that would otherwise not be possible. Spiritual inspiration gives us the courage and breadth of vision to *want* to be that responsible for ourselves and the entire cosmic process that created us. And the simple reason we want to be that responsible is that, first and foremost, we want to be *free*. Free, in this sense, means available. Available means we are no longer endlessly distracted by the karmic momentum of the past, by the fears and desires of the personal ego or the culturally conditioned self. Only when buoyed by a measure of inner freedom from that momentum will we be spiritually awake here and now and therefore available for the overwhelming task of consciously creating the future.

What I am proposing here is an intimidating prospect for most of us. Just ask yourself: Am I ready to take unconditional responsibility for *all* of myself, right now, without excuses? Don't be surprised if you see yourself recoiling, hesitating, grasping for justifications as to why you're not ready just yet.

Why do we experience fear and hesitation at the mere thought of wholeheartedly embracing this kind of responsibility? Because life probably hasn't been a smooth ride. We have suffered. We have all been hurt, to some degree, in our lifetimes, and we carry the memory of that trauma with us. I'm not talking just about childhood wounds here. What I'm pointing to stretches way beyond our personal life-experience. We all carry accumulated cosmic and cultural impressions—memories of pain, suffering, conflict, and chaos that are remnants of our deep-time evolutionary journey. Remember, that trip has not been a peaceful one. The journey from energy to light to matter to life to self-reflective awareness has been a rollercoaster ride, to say the least. From stars imploding into black holes to the fiery birth of our own planet, the journey has been one of explosive violence. The grand emergence and gradual evolution of life from primitive cells to more complex creatures has been a non-stop battle for survival. Can you imagine what it would be like to live in fear of being consumed or torn apart by a wild beast or a neighboring tribe? The majority of human history has been a tale of war and bloodshed. In the same way, higher human development is a messy and complex process, often plagued by emotional and psychological wounds and traumas. The entire journey from the big bang to the present moment is a story of conflict. In fact, that's a fundamental expression of the creative process. So it's understandable that even a highly evolved, sensitive human being would experience, to some degree, a lack of trust in life. It makes sense that there would be, within us, an instinctive unwillingness to trust and to be undefended. But this deep existential mistrust, fear, and suspicion, as reasonable as it may be, is an enormous obstacle to our higher evolutionary aspirations. It is preventing too many of us from stepping forward to embrace the responsibility that we must take if we are to be the ones who will consciously create our future.

My point is that emotional wounds and psychological scars are an almost unavoidable result of our collective developmental process. This is why it is so, so important to come to that point in our own spiritual evolution where we are finally ready and willing to be wholeheartedly accountable for ourselves—for who we are and how we are. Heroically, we must be ready to accept unconditional responsibility for the seen and unseen consequences of everything that has ever happened to us.

I'm not saying that you are responsible for what other people and life may have done *to* you, or for events and circumstances that were beyond your control. I am saying that you need to take responsibility for the *consequences* of those events within yourself. No matter what has happened to you in the past, you cannot allow yourself to take the position of a victim.

As long as you allow yourself to be victimized by your own past wounds and traumas, it is inevitable that sooner or later you are going to wound and traumatize others, and therefore your own past will continue to have negative consequences in the present moment. All kinds of unconscious and conditioned responses naturally arise within us as a result of our personal past and our cultural and biological history, which can, at times, manifest as irrational fears, unfounded aggression, or misplaced resentment. These responses generate a powerful momentum of their own. That's what *karma* is—the accumulated consequences of everything we have done and everything that has happened to us, both positive and negative, experienced deep inside us as a slow but relentless momentum.

Karma can be both positive and negative. Positive karma is the momentum of those actions and consequences that actually cause evolution and higher development to occur. Negative karma is the momentum of those actions and consequences the weight of which inhibit evolution and higher development.

If you don't take responsibility for your own negative karma, it's almost inevitable that you will continue to act out of that mistrust and hesitation, that fear, aggression, and resentment, and most likely end up perpetuating for others the same reality that you have not been willing to put an end to in yourself. That's how the powerful momentum of karma continues to be generated—from person to person, from year to year, from decade to decade, from generation to generation, and even from lifetime to lifetime.

For most of us, negative karma is a powerful force—the accumulated momentum of countless actions motivated by fear, ignorance, and selfishness. Look at your own life. Look at your parents, your family, your friends. Look at the culture around you—at your country or your ethnic group. See how the chain of karma has been handed down. It's simply the law of cause and effect ceaselessly playing itself out in self, culture, and cosmos. As long as you are living and breathing, acting and reacting in this vast interrelated process, there will *always* be cause and effect. It's unavoidable. But the whole point of embracing the Power of Volition is to take responsibility for that unavoidable reality and make it *conscious*.

Unless you sincerely strive to become more conscious, then the past is inevitably going to determine how you act in the present moment. Remember, we all have a measure of freedom in relationship to the choices we make—not absolute freedom, but some degree. And if you accept that truth, that measure of freedom is always enough to make it possible for you to begin to take responsibility for yourself. But if you insist on being a wounded victim, you are choosing to remain oblivious to your choices and their inevitable consequences. And you will use the measure of freedom that is your birthright to do more or less what you have always done, because that's what feels safe and predictable and known. In this way, your choices continue to be driven by unconscious motives arising from unresolved karmic issues, from this life and even from others. Unless a transformative moment arises in your own development when you are finally willing to take responsibility for *all* of your past, without conditions, no matter what the implications, that karmic momentum will not come to an end. If you don't embrace it, it will continue. It always does. And that momentum will determine your choices and your destiny.

The point of Evolutionary Enlightenment is for the best part of you—the Authentic Self—to take the reins not only of your own destiny but also, as audacious as it may sound, the direction of the interior of the cosmos. And you can see that it just would not be possible to take on even a fraction of the burden of cosmic evolution unless you were willing to at least take unconditional responsibility for your *own* karmic burden. How could an unconscious victim be expected to be responsible for evolving the interior of the cosmos? How can any one of us heroically embrace that responsibility and make the right choices if we are hiding out, holding back, fiercely protecting our woundedness?

Of course, some people have experienced such severe trauma and suffering that they are too damaged to take on this kind of radical responsibility. For the rest of us, however, as harsh as it may sound to some, if we really want to create a different future, we have to get over ourselves. After all, in light of the fact that it was you who chose to initiate the entire evolutionary process, what are a few psychological bumps and bruises? In light of the fact that that process is now depending on each and every one of us to create the next step, even the deep scars of ethnic and cultural conflict are no longer valid excuses for holding back. From the biggest perspective, do we really have time to excessively dwell upon the past? If your life-context is merely personal, your psychological, emotional, and cultural wounds can seem overwhelming. But when you see them as a very small part of a very big picture, you'll be able to handle them and keep them in perspective. You will accept that your karma is your responsibility, not anybody else's.

THE POWER AND PURPOSE OF practicing the second tenet is to free the evolutionary process from the burden of your own unresolved negative karma—both personal and cultural. And the way you do that is through taking it all on your own shoulders. You bear it, so that no one else has to suffer its consequences. Heroically, you strive to free the world from the accumulated momentum of your lower impulses, your ego's conditioned fears and desires, and the unenlightened and evolutionarily uninformed values of your cultural past. Most importantly, through doing so, you liberate the best part of yourself—your Authentic Self—to consciously create the future. Only when we are willing to take responsibility for the karmic consequences of everything that has already happened, will we be in a position to shoulder the infinitely greater responsibility for that which has not yet happened. When you liberate the most precious gift evolution has given you—your freedom to choose—from the weight of the past, not only will you cease to create negative karma but you will begin to generate an entirely new, positive, spiritually empowered momentum.

How is that new momentum generated? Through your own choices, through your own volition. When the inspired intention to evolve, which comes from the original creative impulse, is married with your heroic willingness to take unconditional responsibility for your own karmic predicament and your choices, then *conscious evolution* becomes possible. Of course, it's not possible for any one of us to be completely conscious. But if these tenets are taken seriously, if you *live* them, you can become *conscious enough* to make all the difference in the world.

When you use the measure of freedom you have in every moment to actualize your evolutionary potential, dramatic and extraordinary change in the world around you is inevitable. And it's not dependent on anyone but you. You, as a human being, are choosing, through your own higher will, through the Power of Volition, to activate the process of evolution in and through yourself. You become the evolutionary agent.

# CHAPTER 14

# Face Everything and Avoid Nothing

THE THIRD TENET OF EVOLUTIONARY ENLIGHTENMENT is called Face Everything and Avoid Nothing. This tenet points us to our potential to experience unobstructed awareness—awareness that is free from the psychological self-protective habit of avoidance. The liberation of awareness has been the goal of spiritual enlightenment for millennia. And when we see enlightenment in an evolutionary context, this perennial ideal is equally important. It leads to a kind of clarity, transparency, and inner freedom that is the essential foundation for conscious evolution.

Like all the tenets, Face Everything and Avoid Nothing is both the path and the goal. This means that if you have reached the goal, if you are identifying more with your Authentic Self than you are with your ego, then the conscious or unconscious motives within you to avoid this degree of transparency will have been largely transcended. But if you are still identified with ego to a significant degree, then the intentional and deliberate practice of facing everything and avoiding nothing will be the powerful means through which you will gain access to a similar level of spiritual attainment. To the degree that your consciousness is freed from the ego's agenda of narcissistic self-protection and becomes focused on the evolutionary impulse, you will experience the emergence of your own Authentic Self, the nature of which is buoyant, joyful, awake, and future-oriented. In contrast, the ego is absorbed in every moment by its personal fears and concerns, and this obscures your capacity to experience the immediacy of evolutionarily enlightened awareness.

Most of us, with rare exceptions, are deeply invested, consciously or unconsciously, in maintaining the status quo. The ego, both personal and cultural, has numerous emotional, psychological, and historically conditioned agendas that take priority over the evolution of consciousness. The ego is deeply invested in maintaining a certain image of itself and of reality, and will do so at any cost—even if it means avoiding and denying the truth of how things actually are. Therefore, most of us have many reasons to avoid and to deny, to repress and to suppress, to deceive and to conceal. If you have spent a lifetime identified primarily with your ego—with your personal story and with outdated and unenlightened cultural values—it is likely that the posture of avoidance is deeply habitual. Facing everything and avoiding nothing then becomes a powerful path and practice for catalyzing the evolution of consciousness.

If you are bold in your spiritual intention, if you dare to heroically aspire to take responsibility for evolution's next step, you simply cannot afford to have your awareness obscured by the ego's need to avoid. Indeed, for those of us who have awakened to the impulse to evolve, and who understand, at least to some degree, that the destiny of the interior of the cosmos is dependent upon our conscious evolution, cultivating clarity, transparency, and inner freedom becomes a matter of great urgency. If you are deeply committed to this evolutionary endeavor, you will *want* to face everything and avoid nothing, because the last thing you want to do is to act out of some unconscious motive in such a way that would obstruct your own higher development. You practice the third tenet *as if your life depended on it,* because when your life is dedicated to the evolution of consciousness and culture, it does.

Spiritual practice, in one form or another, has always been about the cultivation of awareness. This is why I call Face Everything and Avoid Nothing the ultimate form of spiritual practice. But we need to be prepared for what this practice will reveal. Sincerely engaging with the third tenet inevitably brings to light one of the most notorious faces of the ego: the perennial attachment to pride and self-image.

Doesn't your ego have a particular self-image that it is deeply attached to? It might be a very positive picture, or it might be quite a negative one. It might be a culturally constructed ideal. If you look honestly at your own experience, you will see that it is an image that you work very hard to maintain. How do you maintain it? By filtering out information that conflicts with that picture in any way. What happens when you see something about yourself that doesn't fit neatly with your self-image? You push it away, to the very edge of your awareness, and if you are successful, you banish it altogether. This process is occurring in large and small ways in most of us all the time. Like a camera lens, focusing and refocusing, we constantly frame our own perspective on reality to reflect the picture of ourselves that we want to see.

Ego, in this sense, is a defense mechanism, designed to protect the self from what it feels may be "too much" reality. As long as we are primarily identified with the narrow world of the personal self, the lens of our perception will always be, to some degree, blinded by pride, ever-obstructing our capacity to experience liberated awareness and fearless transparency.

A LIBERATED RELATIONSHIP TO LIFE is one that is no longer dominated by the culturally conditioned desire to maintain the status quo, to preserve the self-image we already hold dear. You recognize that that image creates a barrier, a wall that shields the self from a deeper embrace of reality. Facing everything and avoiding nothing is a powerful tool with which to pierce that barrier, to shatter the ego's defenses in every moment. When you are committed to the aspiration to be liberated, this practice is a source of tremendous energy and inspiration, because in every moment, it has the power to remove the barriers to the emergence of your own Authentic Self.

Even for the most committed spiritual practitioner, facing everything and avoiding nothing is an enormous challenge. Never underestimate the power of the conditioned and often unconscious will to avoid, the tenacity of the ego's investment in its self-image. If you have not yet become clear about the first tenet—about the fundamental issue of what is most important to you—the practice of paying attention won't necessarily help you be more awake. It will just end up being the personal self watching itself, which is like the ego looking in the mirror. You may perform different spiritual practices, which can help you to cultivate awareness, focus, and attention, but only if you want to evolve beyond ego will paying attention have the power to shatter the ever-selective mirror of pride.

As long as we remain invested in the ego's need to manipulate reality, we will find that we keep making the same mistakes, over and over and over again, because we are deliberately avoiding aspects of the way things are. It's not a mystery: if we are trying to get somewhere, but we cover our eyes to avoid seeing the obstacles that lie in our path, it's no wonder we keep tripping over them.

Unless we awaken to a deeper, spiritually inspired conscience, the posture of avoidance easily becomes habitual. This is how it works:

When we first choose—consciously or unconsciously—to avoid something, it may be initially uncomfortable, but very quickly that state of avoidance becomes normal. Deep in our hearts we may know that it's wrong to live in denial of whatever the issue may be, but when we decide that for whatever reason it's just too much to face, we give ourselves license to ignore our own conscience. And before long, it becomes comfortable to remain in that state of denial—in fact, it gets easier and easier. If we don't face things, within hours, if not minutes, the posture of avoidance becomes tolerable. Aren't there times when you experience a kind of numbness in relationship to something you know you should not feel at ease with? Imperceptibly, it just sets in, like ice dulling the pain of an injury, until we feel no discomfort at all.

In this way, slowly but surely, avoidance becomes a habit. Of course, on a spiritual level, a soul level, it's never comfortable. But the point is that when you choose to avoid, you lose touch with your own soul. Emotionally, you become disconnected from your own deeper dimensions. It's as if there is a wall, a barrier, between you and your own authenticity. And far too many of us get accustomed to living like this.

The degree to which we avoid and deny is the degree to which the inner wall of pride that is ego will continue to strengthen. If we are in the habit of constant avoidance, ego becomes hard and impermeable, and every time we choose to avoid something, that wall gets reinforced. Avoidance literally creates ego, and the ego's ability to reinforce its own walls is quite extraordinary. It's not a game—some human beings will go so far as to damage their own souls because they don't want to face themselves. But the moment we stop avoiding, those walls will begin to crumble.

What most of us are unaware of is that every time we choose to avoid, we are holding back the current of the evolutionary impulse, that surge of enlightened energy and intelligence, from working through us. So when you begin to awaken and to intuit that the very purpose of human incarnation is to cooperate with that impulse, to become nothing less than its partner in the creative process, your spiritual obligation is to remove all the barriers to your own potential for higher development by facing everything and avoiding nothing at all times, in all places, under all circumstances.

Always remember: facing everything really does mean *everything*. And if this practice is going to have the power to liberate, it always has to happen now—never tomorrow, or in the future, or at any time other than the present moment. That is what is so powerful about the third tenet: it is the immediacy of its demand that challenges the ego in such a fundamental way. The liberating power of this tenet is only accessed through living it without conditions, always now.

This radical immediacy is what destroys the ego's defenses. The ego always insists that you need more time before you are ready to let go. That's its job—to censor and control your experience, to avoid and postpone, endlessly. If there is integrity in your aspiration to consciously evolve, however, you won't need any more time. When you are committed, the time is always now. Good intentions for the future only flatter the ego. Unless you intend to do it now, you won't do it. When you Face Everything and Avoid Nothing now, you transcend the ego right now. And if you keep facing everything and avoiding nothing, always now, you will transcend the ego in every moment.

As YOU BEGIN TO ENGAGE with this practice, it is important to understand that facing everything and avoiding nothing is a very different practice than assuming the removed position of the witness or observer, as we often do in a meditative posture. In the meditative position, we assume no relationship to the content of consciousness. But when we Face Everything and Avoid Nothing, we choose to have an active relationship with the content of consciousness. When you do this, your soul is undefended, and you will find, as a result, that you not only see a lot more but you also feel a lot more. You are much more sensitive to the extremes and fluctuations of your internal responses.

When you remove the protective shield of avoidance and self-protection, there is an intensity and vulnerability to the human experience. All the complexity of life hits you more directly. So once again, facing everything and avoiding nothing is not merely a state of observing or bearing witness to your own experience. It demands that you be emotionally willing to bear a degree of reality—both in regard to yourself and to life itself—that you may have been unwilling to tolerate before.

When we Face Everything and Avoid Nothing, we become aware of a much broader spectrum of human nature. If we intend to evolve, we have to embrace the emotional and spiritual challenge of facing directly into both the overwhelming brightness of our own highest potentials and the heartless corruption of our darkest motives. Allow yourself to expand the spectrum of possibilities you are willing to see. On one hand, you will glimpse a higher level of glory and goodness than you ever dreamed possible. On the other, you will become more acutely aware of the lower drives in the human psyche—primitive motives and impulses that can be frightening, shocking, and humiliating to the ego's self-image. Because you are facing everything and avoiding nothing, you allow yourself to see it all without recoil, without pride, without resistance.

It takes a very big heart and a truly courageous interest in our collective higher development to bear the entire spectrum of human potential, in and as yourself, without flinching. Most of us unknowingly cling to a self-image that resists extremes—always in denial of our darkness, and ever-fearful of the overwhelming brightness of our unexplored heights. A heroic practice of the third tenet enables you to fearlessly face these extremes—because you want to evolve more than you want to hold on to any particular image of yourself. If you want to be an enlightened person, if you want to evolve beyond individual and cultural ego, if you want to develop your higher human potentials in many dimensions simultaneously, you will find that you are no longer attached to a fixed notion of self. You no longer see yourself as a static entity. You are a work in progress, and because of that, you are no longer so afraid of the truth.

As THE WALLS OF SELF-PROTECTIVE DENIAL and avoidance crumble, you will feel yourself waking up—waking up to the nature of consciousness, waking up to the human experience, waking up to the complex workings of individual and collective development. Your eyes will open wider; you will sit up straight. You will start paying greater attention to your own internal experience, interested in the way changing states of consciousness impact how the world appears to you. You will learn to recognize the many dimensions of the self and understand what causes them to come to the fore or fall back and disappear. You will feel a growing appreciation for the entire spectrum of human nature—from the primitive drives and impulses of our collective evolutionary past to the glorious newly emerging potentials at the leading edge of higher human development. You will start to be able to engage with and cultivate the very best parts of yourself. And you will be aware of unwholesome and destructive impulses when they arise within you and, therefore, will be in a position to take responsibility for them. All of this will emerge in your awareness because you are facing everything and avoiding nothing—because you want to liberate the self from the narrow-minded agendas of your personal ego and the outdated perspectives of the culturally conditioned self so that consciousness will always be free to evolve through you.

When you truly Face Everything and Avoid Nothing, you will no longer be afraid to stand tall—before your own conscience, before others, before God. This is because you are no longer hiding anything from yourself. Through this noble practice, you will cultivate integrity and discover the kind of soul-strength that only comes from fearlessly facing the truth. The instinctive defense mechanisms that the ego hides behind will crumble, and your self and soul will become a transparent vehicle through which the evolutionary impulse can work in this world.

## CHAPTER 15

# The Process Perspective

THE FOURTH TENET OF EVOLUTIONARY ENLIGHTENMENT is called the Process Perspective. It points us directly to the liberating viewpoint that emerges when we see every aspect of our human experience as part and parcel of the vast impersonal cosmic process. The fourth tenet compels us to embrace nothing less than a cosmocentric orientation to life. And most importantly, engaging with this tenet enables us to break through the habit of compulsive personalization that so many of us are painfully trapped in.

Looking through the lens of the fourth tenet, you recognize all events and experiences—both internal and external—to be products of an evolutionary process, and you see all those events and experiences from the perspective of that process rather than from the vantage point of the personal ego. When you fully embrace this perspective, it's as if you become the whole process looking at a very small part of itself, rather than that small part beholding the entire process from afar. It's like seeing everything that occurs from the outside in, as opposed to from the inside out. And this outside-in perspective changes *how* you see *what* you see in a dramatic and liberating way. Now you see what once appeared to be discrete events as being interconnected—all the way from a shooting star in the night sky to a devastating flood to the global economic recession to the sound of a dog barking in the yard to the thrill of meeting a lover after a prolonged separation. All you see is one vast unbroken continuum.

That continuum is the infinitely dense cosmic process that began with the big bang, when everything dramatically burst forth from nothingness. As we have explored in these pages, that process has both an interior dimension and an exterior dimension. The exterior is matter—the Milky Way, Mount St. Helens, Manhattan, your physical body, a fur coat. The interior is your experience of subjectivity, consciousness, self-reflective awareness. It is also emotions like love and fear, the experience of higher cognition, and the mystical feeling of Being.

Through practicing the fourth tenet, we discover the liberating truth that life is not a personal drama but is in fact an impersonal process. This shift of perspective enables us to powerfully penetrate the walls of our separate, personal existence. Ultimately, it reveals that the self is not a unique entity but a process that is a very small part of a larger process, which is part of yet another larger process, and so on. This Process Perspective or "impersonal view," as I used to call it, opens up a portal to enlightened awareness, because it renders transparent that which once appeared solid. It also illuminates the reality that truly nothing is static, that everything is moving, and most importantly, that we're all going somewhere. We're on a moving train. That train is the evolutionary impulse and the tracks are the process it is giving rise to in every moment.

When you contemplate the truth of process and impersonality, you awaken to the transparency of the material world and experience direct access to what is at the heart of evolution and is driving it forward in every moment. In this way, the fourth tenet brings to light the nondual or singular nature of the entire process that is producing the experience you are having in this very moment. It directly reveals the perennial mystical revelation that there is only One—one process, one singular unfolding. Like all the tenets, this fourth one is both the path and the goal.

MANY PEOPLE ARE ATTRACTED TO the notion of cosmic evolution but balk at the word "impersonal." We tend to interpret that term to mean "cold" or "inhuman," but in a cosmocentric context it's actually quite the opposite. I'm not referring to an impersonal process in a mechanical, materialistic sense. This process is *alive*. And it's you. The process is you. What is so important about this shift of perspective is that you see your own sense of self as not separate, at any level, from this vast unfolding stream of development.

Contrary to what you might think when you hear the word "impersonal" or "process," the fourth tenet actually reveals a deeper potential for your own humanity. In fact, because it points you beyond the confines of the separate self and its endless self-concern, the freedom you find there enhances and enlarges to almost infinite proportions your sense of the significance of being human.

Once again, awakening to the Process Perspective has nothing to do with being removed or cold or unfeeling or uncaring. It means transcending the personal world of the separate self to such a degree that you find you care about others, about the world, about the life process itself, in a much deeper and more profound way than you ever imagined possible.

THERE IS NOTHING MORE POWERFUL than this Process Perspective to help us see through the seductive veil of narcissism that has become our personal and cultural predicament. If you have the courage to see beyond the illusion of solidity and separation, the experience is literally enlightening because you directly glimpse your own self beyond ego.

When you apply this perspective to the way you normally relate to yourself and your own experience, it can turn your whole world upside down. Most of us have been brought up to believe that we are unique individuals, that we are special, that there is nobody quite like us. But when you begin to look at your own experience through the lens of the fourth tenet, this conviction gets harder and harder to sustain. When you recognize yourself to be a very small part of a complex, ever-expanding, multidimensional process, and see how almost every aspect of that experience has been produced by what has come before, it becomes increasingly difficult to see yourself as a completely unique individuated entity. This perspective ultimately reveals that the separate self-sense is nothing more than an illusion of uniqueness, created moment by moment through our compulsive habit of personalizing almost every thought, feeling, and sensation we have.

If you think about it, much of the experience that we all have is quite similar. We all experience hope; we all experience fear. We all experience happiness and sadness, inspiration and exhaustion. From the mundane to the miraculous, from the meaningful to the absurd, the majority of our experience generally falls within a common spectrum of possibility. Of course, there are exceptions, and many factors determine which parts of that spectrum show up in the experience of any particular individual. But from the Process Perspective, *none* of it is personal. We awaken to the radically impersonal nature of the very event of experience itself, all the way from the subtle heights of mystical intuition to lower primal impulses like hunger and sexual desire. Why is this important? Because the ego likes to create the illusion that everything that happens to you, from the mundane to the miraculous, is a personal affair—an event that, in some gross or subtle way, *means something about you*.

In this way, the narcissistic separate self creates the appearance of a personal drama with you at center stage. But it's not actually real. In fact, if you step back, you realize that the very capacity to experience that personal drama of "me" has been produced by this vast process. *So even the fact that experience appears to be personal is an impersonal evolutionary phenomenon.* I'm not denying that your experience *feels* personal. Your experience feels personal to you. My experience feels personal to me. The whole point, though, is that even that experience of it feeling personal is completely impersonal. We are a process. *You are a process.* And your process is a small part of a larger process. You cannot stand outside of it. Dare to face this and you will become transparent to yourself.

As you see through the illusion of the personal, you will recognize the truth that who we are as human beings is a bundle of impulses, reactions, and habits, conditioned patterns that together create the convincing appearance of unique individuality. But the truth is that *there isn't anybody in there.* Or, another way of looking at this same picture would be that there is only *One* in there. And that One, the "I" of the cosmos, is the energy and intelligence that initiated the creative process, looking out at its own creation through this particular body, with this particular set of life circumstances, which give rise to certain reactions, responses, preferences, perspectives, interpretations, and so on. It's the same consciousness at the root of all experience; it's the same singularity that's looking out at the world *through* the prism of the conditioned perspective of a particular body and mind. And all of the attributes of that body and mind—its biological nature, its ethnic and cultural background, its personal history, and its emotional and psychological tendencies—are like outer sheaths through which life, the human experience, the world, and the cosmos are seen and interpreted by the one "I."

From the perspective of enlightened awareness, of nonduality, it's the *one I* that is having the whole spectrum of human experiences, through the appearance of relative difference. It's having a physical experience. It's having a male experience or a female experience. It's having a Buddhist experience, a Muslim experience, a Jewish experience, or a Christian experience. It's having an American experience, a Chinese experience, an African experience. It's having a traditional, modern, or postmodern experience.

To most people, the sheer impersonality of this perspective is disconcerting, and it can feel profoundly uncomfortable to the ego, or to any part of the self that is identified with being separate, unique, or special. But if we want to evolve, it's imperative to recognize, at least momentarily, the radical arbitrariness of these differences that we consider to be so personal and so meaningful.

These many sheaths of identity are usually so close to our felt sense of self that it can be enormously challenging to disembed our awareness from their familiar and habitual viewpoints. Releasing your awareness from the unconscious and automatic personalization of biological impulses, psychological tendencies, and cultural biases is spiritual heavy lifting. But if you don't make the heroic effort to do so, you are never going to discover who you are beyond the ego, beyond all relative notions of self. Because of how intimate these multiple layers of relative identity usually feel, you are likely to assume that they are as significant and as personal as they appear to be in any given moment.

Take a moment to reflect on this. If you close your eyes and pay attention, you will notice that there is the feeling sense of being an individual who is having a particular experience, positive or negative. There seems to be a "you" that something is happening *to*. But if you shift your viewpoint away from that individuated self-sense, and step back as far as you can, you will see that from another perspective, *from the outside in*, there's just experience that is occurring. You can recognize that things are just *happening,* more than things are happening *to you*. Seeing in this way—from the perspective of the evolutionary process—is a radical decentralization of your sense of self.

What is it like to be you then, if you are having an identical experience to the one you are having right now—the same sensations, the same thoughts, the same feelings—but none of it is being personalized? The content of your experience doesn't necessarily change, but the *context* of the experience and the sense of who it is happening to changes dramatically.

To deeply grasp the liberating truth that you are not a personal drama but an impersonal process, you will need to practice this shift of perspective over and over again. You may glimpse it for a moment, but for the Process Perspective to have the power to liberate your awareness, you need to make the noble effort to look through this lens every day. We all already know what our experience looks like through the lens of the ego's conditioned habit of personalization, but this fourth tenet points to a very different and less familiar way to see the human experience.

It takes courage and humility to let in how much of what you consider to be uniquely you has actually been shaped by the evolutionary process and the world around you. Your physical form follows a pattern that has been forged by life conditions in the exterior world—by genetics, by the natural environment—over millions of years. Your inner life—the patterns of your emotional and psychological experience—has been largely shaped by the interior world, by the values of your family, the historical belief structures of your race or ethnic group, and the ideas you may have absorbed from your culture. Even the thoughts and feelings that are arising in your awareness at this very moment reflect emotional, psychological, and cultural structures or habits that have slowly developed over tens of thousands of years. This is all part of the deep-time developmental process that emerged from the big bang.

When your own perspective shifts in this way, and you see through the eyes of the "I" of the cosmos, your relationship to your own experience can change dramatically. If you want to become an evolutionarily enlightened person, this is a perspective that needs to be cultivated until it becomes habitual.

WHEN YOU AUTHENTICALLY TRANSCEND the ego's personal drama and discover the truth of the impersonal process, the personal sphere of your life does not cease to exist. The fourth tenet is more subtle than that. As I have been saying, there are different dimensions or levels of the self, different sheaths through which the one "I" becomes manifest. Our experience of the personal sphere is the primary filter through which we see and engage with the world around us. But the whole point of the fourth tenet is the recognition that who you are and who I am is not *limited* to that personal sphere. When you discover this enlightening truth, it will change the way you interpret and respond to all of the many different dimensions of your humanity: the biological urges, the memories, thoughts and emotions, and the culturally conditioned tendencies that arise within you. They will not go away, or necessarily even lessen in intensity. And you may choose to respond to them or not. But if you can see the personal sphere from the perspective of an impersonal cosmic process, there will be *space* around the arising of those impulses—a newfound space in which you can make appropriate choices, informed by a greater context.

That's what the Process Perspective is: a *bigger context*. From this perspective, you see your personal experience, which at times can feel overwhelming, within an infinitely larger context. The drama of your personal desires and concerns is, if not irrelevant, always secondary to the prime directive of the Authentic Self, which is the evolution of the process itself. When you are lit up by the evolutionary impulse, there are times when its creative passion completely overshadows personal concerns that, in other contexts, might appear to be profoundly significant.

It can indeed be a disconcerting experience to simultaneously hold in awareness all of these dimensions or levels of your own self—to feel at one level deeply connected to the personal sphere, to your intimate and historical relationships, your culture, ethnicity, and unique personality, and yet at another level to feel no relationship to anything personal whatsoever. Both of those experiences are real, but they are different dimensions of the self. And we tend to be much more familiar with the world of the ego or personal self than we are with the cosmic context and identity of the Authentic Self. In our culture, in which the rights, needs, and significance of the individual tend to be held most sacred, the personal dimension has become imbued with exaggerated importance. We have become conditioned to seek the deepest connection to life primarily through the personal sphere, and, therefore, it is a profound step forward when we gain the ability to see this dimension of our experience in a context that infinitely transcends it.

$$\oplus$$

As we evolve, we will find that our conditioned attachment to and personalization of relative notions of self will gradually diminish. There will be a decreasing emotional and psychic investment in lesser dimensions of who we are, and simultaneously there will be a growing emotional connection to a cosmic sense of identity. As your capacity to see through the eyes of the one "I" increases over time, you will experience a loosening of your identification with the relative sheaths.

A thrilling shift of identity begins to occur. And to me, what is most significant about this shift is that as you identify more and more deeply with the Authentic Self and its cosmic aspirations, slowly but surely *what feels personal to you begins to change*. What becomes a personal matter *is* the evolution of consciousness. You *feel* more deeply connected to that vast impersonal process than you do to your so-called personal life. When you authentically make this leap beyond the personal, your emotional inclinations evolve. You find yourself spontaneously beginning to identify, at a feeling level, with the Authentic Self's passion for conscious evolution above all else. Does this mean you will cease to care about your personal relationships, your connection to your ethnic roots, or the culture from which you have come? No. But it *does* mean that something else has become *more important* to you, because the context for the life you are living has dramatically expanded and deepened.

As we identify with that impersonal energy and intelligence that is driving the creative process, we will find that a higher, spiritually inspired passion and care *does* begin to inform and transform our personal life, our intimate relationships, and the culture we share and cocreate with others. We are all multidimensional beings—simultaneously expressions of the God-impulse *and* embodied, living, breathing humans. And as we awaken to our own higher dimensions and spiritual capacities, we begin to understand that our embodied, conscious engagement with life and with each other *is* the interior of that vast cosmic process evolving. Nothing is ever outside of it. That's the Process Perspective.

# CHAPTER 16

# Cosmic Conscience

THE FIFTH TENET OF EVOLUTIONARY ENLIGHTENMENT, Cosmic Conscience, represents the fundamental motive or *raison d'être* of the evolutionary impulse or Authentic Self. Remember, that impulse gave rise to this entire life-process, and when it awakens in our own hearts and minds, we find that we care passionately about only one thing: *evolution*. In that impulse, there is no other motive than to create the future, unceasingly, and the needs and desires of any individual are always secondary to that greater purpose. This one-pointed passion is what awakens in you as spiritual aspiration, and through the practice of each of the tenets, you align yourself more closely with its forward-reaching momentum.

The fifth tenet signifies a tipping point in the path and practice of Evolutionary Enlightenment—an inner threshold that, once crossed, changes everything. It points to that moment in your own evolution when you begin to care more about the process as a whole than you care about your ego's fears, desires, or concerns. It represents the essential shift of identity that this teaching rests on: the shift from ego to Authentic Self. When this occurs, your very motive for pursuing enlightenment evolves from a fundamentally self-centered motive to one that is focused upon the evolution of consciousness itself.

Once again, the kind of care that this tenet points to is not a practice or a technique—it is the natural or inherent motive of your Authentic Self. But until you have crossed the threshold where that motive becomes your own *raison d'être*, the deliberate and intentional contemplation of what this tenet points to is an essential part of the path, because it puts everything else in context.

⊕

WHEN WE EMBARK ON THE SPIRITUAL QUEST, most of us, understandably, are pursuing freedom or enlightenment for our own sake. This is why we begin by asking, *What do I really want? What is more important to me than anything else?* But once your intention has become clear, and you sincerely pursue that one-pointed aspiration, a profound shift occurs. Over time, as your soul develops and matures through the practice of the first three tenets, you will see the quality of that intention evolve. And as you embrace the fourth tenet, and learn to see yourself as a very small part of a very big process, your relationship to the spiritual path becomes dramatically recontextualized. You discover that it is not about you.

As your understanding and experience grow, you will come to realize that spiritual evolution is not a personal matter. Indeed, to the seeker who is becoming a finder, it becomes more and more apparent that the felt aspiration for spiritual freedom is nothing less than the vibration of the larger evolutionary process awakening to itself within the human heart and mind. In this, you recognize that the pursuit of enlightenment could never have been merely for yourself alone. Remember, fourteen billion years ago, something burst out of nothing, and the leading edge of that miraculous surge of Becoming is found in your own interior, experienced as the emerging capacity for higher consciousness. That's the purpose of enlightenment: to liberate that glorious as-yet-unmanifest evolutionary potential.

THE FIFTH TENET IS THE ONLY ONE of these five tenets that cannot really be practiced in and of itself. The deeper motive it points to emerges authentically as a result of sincerely practicing the other four tenets. If you wholeheartedly pursue your own Clarity of Intention, take unconditional responsibility for your Power of Volition, fearlessly Face Everything and Avoid Nothing, and cultivate a Process Perspective, you will become aware of a spontaneously arising sense of Cosmic Conscience—a care for the vast evolutionary process of which you now know you are a small but significant part. And you will recognize that your own spiritual development, your liberation from individual and collective ego, is absolutely essential for the evolution of the interior dimension of that process. This is why your motive becomes: *I want to be free not for my own sake but for the sake of the whole.* That is the awakening of Cosmic Conscience.

When this becomes your own primary motivation for seeking liberation, something very significant has occurred. What began as a freely made choice has become a choiceless obligation. Your fundamental motive has evolved from one that is essentially self-serving to one that is not separate from the very motive behind the expanding universe—the pure passion of the big bang, the God-impulse, which is your Authentic Self.

This shift of motive is the key to everything. It's amazing what profound transformations can occur when human beings awaken to a larger context and a higher motive than the fears and desires of their own egos. We are all capable of greatness when we feel directly connected to a higher purpose. Think about the human virtues that emerge, for example, in times of war—the heroism, selflessness, generosity of spirit, and risk-taking that are often expressed when a group of individuals bond together in order to defend themselves, their families, their country, and their values from an external threat. That kind of crisis can bring out the best in us. In an instant, our narcissism and petty self-concern can vanish—not because we are trying to improve ourselves but because we have been shocked awake to a bigger picture. Often people who return from war report that despite all the horrors, it was the best time of their life. They discovered what it was to be *awake*, living on the edge, fueled by the ultimacy of a life-and-death context. Imagine what it would be like if a significant number of us felt that same sense of urgency in relationship to our collective spiritual evolution, to the need to develop at the level of consciousness. The change we would be capable of would be dramatic.

Now, of course, in times of war, the primary motive is survival and the goal is the restoration of peace and security. When our fundamental sense of identity shifts to the evolutionary impulse, we are motivated by a similar sense of urgency, only now, our objective is not peace, or physical survival, or emotional and psychological comfort. In an evolutionary context, the goal is not peace; it's *perpetual development*. Evolutionary Enlightenment is inspired by the ecstasy that compels us to create the future. And it's not a future that's going to unfold by itself while we go back to sleep. It's a future that we forge the hard way through direct, conscious, intentional engagement with the life-process.

What is it that will inspire us to find the courage and the heart to take our lives this seriously, to get to that point where we are motivated by the overwhelming urgency of the call of the future? It's difficult to get human beings to feel as passionate about the imperative to evolve as they would feel if their life was being threatened. But that's what Evolutionary Enlightenment is calling us to. And the fifth tenet points to that all-important threshold in our own consciousness and conscience where we begin to care *that* much.

⬒

WHEN YOUR MOTIVE EVOLVES in the way I'm describing, the spiritual impulse becomes the stronger part of who you are, more powerful than your ego's motives. Your spiritually awakened conscience and your passion to create that which is new become much more influential than your attachment to the status quo of your culturally conditioned values, beliefs, and perspectives. And it's important to appreciate what a profound shift this represents in the balance of power within you—the struggle for dominion over your body, mind, and soul.

When that shift from ego to Authentic Self occurs, it is unmistakable and it changes everything. And yet *how it happens* can seem like an ever-impenetrable mystery. *What makes human beings evolve beyond ego?* When exactly does that balance tip, so that an individual's center of gravity moves to a higher level, no longer centered in the fears and desires of the personal self? This can be a confusing question. What I've discovered is that there is actually a science to how this seemingly miraculous shift takes place. The science of radical spiritual transformation comes down to what I sometimes call "the magic number": fifty-one percent.

That's the secret: *Only when the Authentic Self becomes more than fifty-one percent of who you identify yourself to be does the balance shift.* On first

161

hearing, that may sound like an overly simplistic approach, but this is quite a profound revelation. This equation sheds light on the most important question for anyone who wants to embody the evolutionary impulse in this lifetime. It explains that the fundamental shift in motive occurs when, and *only* when, the fearless, passionate, evolutionary idealism of the Authentic Self becomes the greater part of who you are, at a conscious *and unconscious* level.

Remember, the Authentic Self or evolutionary impulse is the part of you that already has *absolutely no doubt* it wants to be free or enlightened more than anything else. In fact, that part of you is *already perfectly free*. But it is also experienced as the part of you that *aspires* toward unqualified freedom. Why? Because you are still divided. To the self-sense that remains primarily identified with ego, the inherently free Authentic Self is experienced as a *desire* for that which you ultimately already are but haven't deeply realized yet. Until you reach that point where your primary locus of identification shifts from the ego to the Authentic Self, your experience will still be, to some degree, one of separation from that which you long for. Only when you make that all-important shift of identity will the state of inherent freedom, which is the already present condition of the Authentic Self, finally be recognized to be that which you always have been. Until you reach that point, you will experience it to be your highest aspiration. When you are spiritually inspired, that's the part of you that wakes up and *knows* something miraculous is possible—the passionate idealism that you feel surging through your system.

Consistent, meaningful, and demonstrable transformation *only* occurs when the individual's awakening to the Authentic Self crosses the threshold from fifty to fifty-one percent. Otherwise, you can experience an awakening to higher potentials, and taste the thrill of the evolutionary impulse stirring within, but as long as the motives of the individual and collective ego remain stronger within you, sooner or later the clarity and conviction and inspiration you find will become a possession of your ego. You may find access to mystical intuitions, feel deeper sentiments and emotions, and even have glimpses of enlightened awareness, and yet all those qualities will be hijacked by your ego if that is where your identity is still rooted.

When that line is finally crossed, however, when the balance of power shifts, the ego becomes the weaker part of the self, and that is what changes everything. So the initial goal, the primary target in this teaching, is to get you so inspired by your own potential and by the urgency of our collective predicament that you are willing to do *whatever* you need to do in order to cross that threshold. And once again, the way you do that is to embrace the first four tenets—making spiritual evolution your highest priority; taking unconditional responsibility for yourself; facing everything and avoiding nothing; and cultivating a process perspective. Each of these aligns you with the position of the already liberated Authentic Self, which only wants to evolve, *already* feels responsible, has no motive to avoid, and recognizes itself to be the source of the entire evolutionary unfolding. And in this way, you can slowly but surely tip the balance of power within yourself, until you cross the fifty-one-percent threshold.

When this all-important shift occurs, the fears and desires and aspirations of the personal ego and cultural self will have been displaced to a significant degree—at least fifty-one percent—by the unstoppable drive of the evolutionary impulse. Now it is Eros, the powerful urge and creative spark driving the entire evolutionary process, which has become the dominant intelligence and energy within your own self. You will start to feel a growing momentum, a backdraft propelling you forward, because when the Authentic Self is the dominant presence in your being, you feel directly connected to the source of the creative impulse. You are no longer running merely on the fuel of your own will and intention; there is now a deeper and higher motive, a cosmic energy and intelligence that is catapulting you forward.

However, crossing the fifty-one-percent threshold is not the end of the path—it is just the beginning. As you take that step, the ego doesn't just disappear, or even lie down quietly. If it continues to represent as much as forty-nine percent of your self-sense, then you still have a long way to go. But because the balance of power within yourself has tipped from the ego to the Authentic Self, you begin to experience a tremendous sense of obligation and what I call evolutionary tension. You realize you simply *cannot* continue to live for your own sake alone; indeed, you awaken to the moral imperative to ensure that the process evolves through you.

This obligation is Cosmic Conscience. And the degree to which you awaken to this emerging moral imperative is the degree to which you will actually find the wherewithal to handle your own ego. However overwhelming its fears and desires may be at times, you will know that who you really are and what you're here for is far greater than any of those personal concerns. That alone is what makes it possible to abandon your attachment to and investment in many of the relative and sometimes unwholesome expressions of self and embrace the ultimately empowering and ennobling qualities of natural dignity, humility, and self-respect that Cosmic Conscience engenders in the human heart and soul.

⊕

THE EMERGENCE OF COSMIC CONSCIENCE is very significant, not only for your own higher development but in relationship to the evolution of our shared culture. From a certain point of view, the evolution of culture can be described as the gradual widening of our circles of care and concern for something greater than ourselves—from ego-centric to ethnocentric to worldcentric and beyond. In ethnocentric and traditional cultures, for example, everybody cares about *our* survival. If you are part of a close-knit tribe, religious group, or community, you feel a sense of solidarity. Everyone is there for each other in the face of a perceived threat, but the circle of care and concern is still quite localized.

The fifth tenet points to a much wider circle than that, wider even than a worldcentric care, in which we feel a sense of responsibility for the welfare of all our fellow humans and the plight of our shared planet. In the fifth tenet, we experience a felt sense of cosmocentric care, which is more identified with the evolutionary process as a whole than with any lesser notions of self. Indeed, now you awaken to a sense of care for *consciousness* and where it is headed, because your sense of self is no longer merely related to your own family, your fellow Jews or Christians, Americans or Chinese. This is what uniquely emerges at a cosmocentric level of development: a felt sense of ecstatic urgency about the evolution of consciousness itself. When you feel this at an emotional level, it's quite a significant evolutionary event with profound implications for where our shared culture is headed.

How often in your life have you experienced caring about the emergence of that which is higher more than you care about anything personal? This kind of cosmocentric care is not related to your ego, and it's not related to your ethnic background, to your traditional religious orientation, or to your culture. It comes from a deeper, higher part of yourself that is *free* from all the lesser though very real dimensions of who you already are. When you start to emotionally respond to life from that part of yourself, something extraordinary has begun to happen.

WHEN YOU ARE LIVING THE FIFTH TENET, when you embrace a cosmo-centric perspective, the world of the Authentic Self becomes the world you live in. You may still exist and function in the ego's world, but that's not your home anymore. And the idea of living "for a higher purpose" almost doesn't make sense once you cross that line, because at an interior level, you and that purpose have merged. It's no longer external to who you are but has become the very source of your sense of self. To a significant degree, you and that higher purpose are indistinguishable. That's what Cosmic Conscience means. Your entire life becomes permeated by the future-oriented passion of the evolutionary impulse, because that is who you have become.

When that pure passion becomes your own passion, your life becomes ennobled—it becomes an expression of the holy life, the spiritual life, a life of meaning and value. You feel as if you have come home and have found your place in the whole matrix of the cosmos. You know who you are and why you are here. As long as your fundamental motive is personal and self-centered, life will never deeply make sense. But when you embrace a higher motive that transcends the personal sphere, every moment becomes infused with a powerful sense of purpose.

As you awaken to the vast dimensions of your own cosmic identity, you find that naturally you care about the future of that process more than you care about your own happiness, or even your own enlightenment. And to your surprise, you will find that, in the end, it is really this care, above all else, that liberates you from ego, because as a result, you find yourself remarkably and quite spontaneously less preoccupied with and less burdened by your personal fears and desires. The ego's petty self-concern is displaced because you are no longer living for your own sake but are now living for the sake of the whole, consumed by a passion to be utterly free so that nothing will inhibit your ability to participate wholeheartedly in the evolutionary process.

When a purpose that is so much deeper and higher than yourself comes into your everyday awareness, you simply don't have the energy for those fears and concerns any more. You become so consumed by the ecstatic nature of the evolutionary impulse, by its dynamism and inherent, explosive freedom, that your ego's self-concern and your culturally conditioned ideas and beliefs no longer have the power to distract you in any significant way. Something infinitely more important has entered the center of your being, and your heart is captivated by that. In this way, your personal liberation becomes merely a spontaneous byproduct of your care for the evolutionary process itself.

This is how, in Evolutionary Enlightenment, the transcendence of ego is achieved. Ego is full of narcissistic self-importance, but it never wants to take on the burden of this kind of awe-inspiring responsibility for evolution, because in so doing it loses its freedom to act in its own self-interest. Awakening to Cosmic Conscience implicates you in the most profound and dramatic way. It says, "The universe is depending on *you*." And this is why it has the power to completely unseat the ego in a way that I don't think anything else can. The irony, in this case, is that this does not happen in the traditional way, through awakening, in mystical revelation, to the fact of your personal insignificance. In this new enlightenment, ego is transcended through seeing quite the opposite: your cosmic *significance*. The solution to the exaggerated sense of self-importance that afflicts most of us is not to feel less important but to discover and take responsibility for just how important you *really* are. There is no greater challenge to narcissism than awakening to Cosmic Conscience: to the fact that *the evolution of the interior of the cosmos is depending on you.*

That is why this tenet is the ultimate solution to the postmodern predicament of narcissism and exaggerated self-importance. You start out on the spiritual path thinking, "I want liberation for myself—I want to become an enlightened human being." But sooner or later, for anyone who seriously pursues that intention in an evolutionary context, you will come to a point where it is glaringly obvious that there is something infinitely bigger than your own personal spiritual aspirations that is calling you. It's no longer "I want that" but rather, "That wants me." And that is a truly religious feeling—an authentic religious sentiment in a completely post-traditional context. That's the beauty of it: the over-inflated postmodern ego always wants for itself, and the only thing that can really turn the tables on its unending craving is the startling recognition that the very thing you were seeking wants everything from you. It turns your whole world upside down. I can't imagine anything that could be more appropriate or more liberating for those of us at the leading edge at this pivotal moment in our culture's unfolding. And I can't imagine anything more desperately needed for the evolutionary process than for a small but not insignificant number of us to cross this momentous threshold.

**PART IV**

# Enlightenment and the Evolution of Culture

# INTRODUCTION TO PART IV

THE PATH AND PRACTICE OF EVOLUTIONARY ENLIGHTENMENT, when embraced with great seriousness and urgency, can catalyze a profound transformation in the individual. Through living the five tenets that I have laid out in Part III of this book, the shift from ego to Authentic Self can occur in a tangible and unmistakable way. When any individual takes the significant step beyond the self-limiting structures of personal history and cultural conditioning, awakening to a deeper and higher sense of Self, it is a profound event. That's what enlightenment has always been about: the experience of consciousness beyond ego. But in the teaching of *Evolutionary* Enlightenment, we are not interested in ego-transcendence as an end in itself. It is a *means* to something far more significant: the evolution of our culture.

This teaching points to the thrilling possibility of a shared experience and expression of higher consciousness, beyond ego boundaries—a way of relating that is so far from our cultural status quo that it is almost impossible to imagine. This is the call of the future. This is the new enlightenment that I am endeavoring to bring into being. Evolutionary Enlightenment is more than an individual attainment; it is a *cultural emergence*. And it occurs when individuals awaken simultaneously to the evolutionary impulse, the energy and intelligence that created the universe.

In this final section, we will explore the dynamics and principles that drive this new cultural potential, and lean into the barely emerging intuitions of what lies just beyond the edge of evolution.

# CHAPTER 17

# A Higher We

THE ULTIMATE GOAL OF EVOLUTIONARY ENLIGHTENMENT is to come together with others in an egoless culture, free from all the usual obstructions to our higher creative potentials and capacities. This is a very bold and noble aspiration, one that is much higher than most of us would even consider reaching for. But when you awaken to the Authentic Self, you will find that it becomes your natural inclination. Indeed, when that powerful energy and intelligence begins to surge through your body and mind, you will find that you are spontaneously drawn to come together with others—others who are awakening to that same spiritual impulse, who share its sense of purpose, urgency, and passion. And why is it that we feel compelled toward higher relatedness in this way? Because that is the nature of the impulse itself.

In traditional enlightenment, which is about awakening to timeless, formless Being, there is no such thing as relatedness, because there is only One. But in Evolutionary Enlightenment, when the emphasis shifts from Being to Becoming, one wholeheartedly enters the world of time, form, and relatedness. In fact, one discovers that relatedness is the whole point of the manifest world. *The universe was created so that relationship could occur.* Why else would God, or the energy and intelligence that initiated this process, have ever left the timeless singularity of the ground of Being? Before the big bang, in that empty ground, there was only unbroken Oneness. But that One chose to become the many, and in the birth of the many, relatedness became the very fabric of the emerging universe.

Indeed, one way to understand the evolutionary impulse is as a desire for *perfect relatedness*—an overwhelming urge to make manifest its ultimate nature as seamless unity in the realm of multiplicity. So when you experience that impulse as the compulsion to evolve, the direction in which it is pointing you is always toward ever more profound expressions of its own inherent singularity, or nonduality. You find yourself mysteriously and miraculously and ecstatically compelled by it. That's why you feel drawn to others—because the evolutionary impulse is drawn to *itself.*

When the evolutionary impulse meets itself, there is egoless *relatedness.* And that is what those of us at the leading edge who want to push the boundaries of our own spiritual development need to discover. We have to find a way to meet one another in a place we've never been before, in a higher state of consciousness and a higher stage of development that are unhindered by the separating influence of the narcissistic ego and the less enlightened values of our modern and postmodern culture. Anyone can experience egoless consciousness in the stillness and solitude of deep meditation. It is easy to be egoless when there's no relationship. But if we want to catalyze evolution in consciousness and culture, we are going to have to *share* our deepest convictions and spiritual intuitions of what's possible, and then work hard, together, to make that possibility a reality. In order to do this, we need to make the heroic effort to go beyond ego at the same time, while we are creatively interacting with one another, in the midst of all the complexity of human life.

WHEN MANY INDIVIDUALS SIMULTANEOUSLY EMBRACE the path and practice I've been describing, and make the all-important shift from ego to Authentic Self, this is what becomes possible. When this happens, consciousness beyond ego, which is enlightenment, can emerge not just within your own individual interior, but *between us,* as human beings. What has traditionally been a subjective experience now becomes an *intersubjective* experience—a new expression of enlightened awareness that emerges in the space *between subjects.*

That space is the interior of the cosmos. The interior of the cosmos is not just inside your own head—it's something we share. That's what intersubjective means. It is the "we-space" in which we share values, perspectives, beliefs, and worldviews. It is culture. Culture is the expression of our collective interior—the invisible structures that exist in that intersubjective domain. These conscious and unconscious, mutually agreed upon beliefs, values, and perspectives are embedded in our language, our customs, and our social systems.

Most of the time, the cultural or intersubjective worldspace we share has little to do with higher evolutionary values or enlightened awareness. It tends to be conditioned by a conglomeration of beliefs and perspectives that come from both our current modern and postmodern cultural experience and from our past, our ethnic roots, and our traditional heritage. Our collective interior, more often than not, has little room for that which is new. Our complex emotional and psychological worldspace is made up largely of what has already happened and what already exists.

When you transcend the outdated beliefs and values of our shared history, and use your gifts of self-reflective awareness and free agency to activate new and higher potentials within yourself, something of greater significance than your own personal awakening can occur. Indeed, when you come together with others who are endeavoring

175

to transcend history in the same way, *cultural evolution* starts occurring through you and between you. Nothing is more spiritually intoxicating than this: when you feel your own interior actually moving, forward and upward, in a context in which others are moving in the same trajectory at the very same time.

In this way, a momentum is generated in consciousness—a vertical momentum toward that which is new. When that momentum is generated, you realize that you are *going somewhere*—and not just as an individual, or even as a collective. In a small but not insignificant way, culture itself is moving. When you know this is possible and then you experience it, directly, it's like discovering the key that unlocks the door to the future. When you feel that shared interior moving and vibrating with a sense of direction, you *know* it is possible to change the world, because the world starts within.

This is why I sometimes speak about Evolutionary Enlightenment as *changing the world from the inside out.* Changing the world means creating the underlying structures for a new level, or stage, of cultural development. Those structures are something we have to build together, in that intersubjective dimension, in the space between subjects.

My vision of a new world is not some vague utopian ideal a thousand years away; it's a new structure in consciousness that emerges between us, in the most interior dimension of the cosmos, in real time, right now. At first, it is glimpsed as a new potential, then tasted as a thrilling intersubjective experience of consciousness beyond the familiar boundaries of the individual ego and the outdated structures of the culturally created self. Eventually, if each of the individuals involved has the heroic commitment necessary to sustain the perspective revealed in that experience, that perspective becomes an actual structure in our shared culture. As it stabilizes, that structure becomes the ground for new and higher orders of relatedness.

THESE NEW AND HIGHER ORDERS of relatedness are hard to conceive of, because they are outside of our usual frame of reference. Imagine what it would be like if there was no sense of *otherness* when you were with other people. How would it feel if there was no trace of self-consciousness, and no preoccupation with superiority, competition, fear, mistrust, or unworthiness? Dare to consider, just for a moment, the possibility of being so at ease in the company of others that there was nothing to hide, nothing to defend, only the fearless transparency of egoless awareness and the ecstatic urgency of the evolutionary impulse. That is what it feels like when we awaken to the Authentic Self, *together*.

The experience of egoless unity or oneness has always been the highest spiritual ideal. The problem, as I've said, is that usually we can sustain the awareness of absolute unity only in a state of solitary meditation or quietude—when the mind is very still and awareness is unmoving, when the many disappear and dissolve into the immanent oneness of consciousness itself. When we emerge from that state and become aware of the many, we usually lose touch with the awareness of the One.

Imagine what would happen, however, if many individuals were able to remain conscious of that absolute unity *while creatively engaging in the world of multiplicity*. Imagine if you could have that same experience of *One without a second* with your eyes open—not immersed in stillness, withdrawn from the world, but passionately engaged with other people and with the life-process. In this way, the experience of nonduality emerges in the space *between* you and others, so that although you are relating, as many, you experience yourselves as One. And that One is a vast unfolding process that is *going somewhere*.

WHEN THE CONSCIOUSNESS OF ONE is shared by two, or ten, or thirty, or more, you experience a kind of intimacy that may surprise and even shock you. What you are meeting those other individuals in has nothing to do with the kind of personal intimacy that the ego can relate to, and nothing to do with the familiar ways in which our culture has taught us to seek for connection with other people.

In earlier stages of our cultural development, we experienced intimate connection with those in our family, our tribe, our religious group, or our nation. In our current modern and postmodern context, we tend to seek for intimacy primarily in romantic relationships, in personal friendships, and in nuclear families. For most of us, trust and intimacy is always a result of sharing experience with others, over time. In the mutual awakening to the Authentic Self, we discover, to our amazement, a new and radical form of intimacy that has nothing to do with time or shared history. In fact, it has nothing to do with anything personal whatsoever. When two or more people awaken to the evolutionary impulse, and glimpse the singular nature of the infinite vastness that is the cosmocentric perspective, there is simply no sense of *otherness*. Even though you can be aware of the objective fact that there is one person here and another person there, emotionally that distinction is not experienced. There is no felt sense of duality, gross or subtle.

When two or more individuals come together in this way and have a conversation, the experience is almost of thinking out loud with yourself, because there is only one Authentic Self. The ego can only have relationships with other separate individuals, but the Authentic Self can only have a relationship with itself. If you awaken to the Authentic Self and another person awakens to that same self, you will feel a strong pull to come together, but interestingly, what you are drawn to is not the other individual's unique personal qualities. You are drawn to the very same evolutionary aspiration that is awakening within you. The Authentic Self isn't interested in other individuals. It is always only interested in *itself* in others.

In that shared higher state, carried by the evolutionary impulse, there is an ecstatic intimacy that cannot be surpassed. It is a sweetness that is infinitely deeper than the experience of sexual union, personal friendship, familial connection, or ethnic bonds. It is not separate individuals coming together; it is one Self delighting in consciously recognizing itself.

⊕

IN THIS NEWLY EMERGING intersubjective enlightenment, the meaning and significance of nonduality *evolves.* That same singularity we taste in deepest Being is now experienced in time, in the body, in action, in Becoming, and most importantly, in relationship. It's what I sometimes call "intersubjective evolutionary nonduality."

Nonduality, once again, means oneness or not-two-ness. Intersubjective means *between subjects,* between individuals. And evolutionary means it is not static or fixed, but perpetually developing. So intersubjective evolutionary nonduality, to put it simply, means *One between two, evolving.* It means the experience of Oneness in a context of dynamic, perpetually developing relatedness. When two or more individuals discover the truth of Oneness through awakening to the Authentic Self, in the same place and the same space, the timeless paradox of nonduality enters the stream of time and becomes the evolving context for a new cultural emergence.

To me, there is nothing more profound than this. If God is that One without a second, then the human experience of intersubjective evolutionary nonduality is the most culturally significant expression of what God actually is for those of us at the leading edge of the evolving world. When a number of apparently separate individuals are liberated from the familiar boundaries of the individual ego and the outdated structures of the culturally created self, the One surges through the many, and the many know that they are the One, and there is a dynamic evolutionary dance between them.

Remember, what is occurring here is always far greater than any of the individuals present. The energy and intelligence that created the universe is drawing human beings together for its *own* purpose. And our personal spiritual aspirations, our connections with each other and with life itself, whether we know it or not, are simply serving that purpose, which is the perpetual evolution of the interior of the cosmos.

## CHAPTER 18

# Catalyzing Emergence

EVOLUTIONARY ENLIGHTENMENT, AND THE NEW CULTURE it promises, is something we can deliberately and consciously bring into being, if we care deeply enough about the potential it is pointing to. But it is not something that can be manufactured simply through sitting in a circle and practicing a certain technique or by generating a particular emotional state. It is an *emergent* perspective, or state of consciousness, that bursts forth spontaneously and miraculously when the conditions are right. *Emergent* means that it is something greater than the sum of the parts—a new *order* of relatedness, a new *level* of consciousness, a deeper and higher perspective that is always unimaginable until the moment it explodes into existence.

The notion of emergence is key to understanding Evolutionary Enlightenment. This teaching is about catalyzing the miracle of emergence in the *interior* of the cosmos, in and through our own selves. So we need to deeply understand how emergence works, and what we can do to ensure that it occurs.

Emergence is not simply the improvement of what already exists; it is the arising of something entirely *new*. It's not just horizontal expansion or modification; it's *vertical* development and growth. When I talk about verticality, it means the emergence of capacities and ways of thinking that are genuinely, authentically new and that did not exist before. It's not the same as a horizontal path, where we are modifying or improving, often in positive and important ways, the self that we already are. Verticality, in Evolutionary Enlightenment, means we engage with the spiritual process in such a way that the result is the emergence of some quality, ability, or capacity that was not there before.

Emergence happens at every level of the evolutionary process. At the beginning of time, something came from nothing. With every step of this vast unfolding, that same mystery is taking place—greater degrees of complexity are emerging from lesser degrees of complexity. This process takes place in matter, in biological life, and, as we are discovering, in the inner dimensions of our own consciousness and shared culture.

If we are interested in learning how to engage with consciousness at higher and higher levels, to consciously facilitate its evolution within us and between us, we need to look more closely at the extraordinary phenomenon of emergence in matter, in biological life, and most importantly, at the level of consciousness. We need to cultivate our capacity to visualize and to emotionally connect with what it would mean for emergence to occur within our own interiors, within our subjective and intersubjective experience.

Emergence is a relatively new concept. How does greater complexity emerge out of lesser complexity? How did something come from nothing? How did all the matter in the universe emerge from primordial emptiness? That's the mystery of life, the mystery of the creative process. Look at the evolution of biological life. Life emerged out of inanimate matter. It started as single-celled organisms, which eventually gave rise to multi-celled organisms, which eventually, over long periods of time, gave rise to all the extraordinary complexity and diversity of sentient life on this planet.

The same process of ever-greater complexification has occurred in the dimension of consciousness. But this is relatively uncharted territory, because it's not yet culturally accepted that evolution is an *internal* as well as an external event. From our contemporary cultural perspective, evolution happens "out there"—in the cosmos, in nature, in biological processes. But when you realize that this process is also unfolding inside you, and even more importantly, *inside us*, that's when the magic starts happening.

When you literally begin to feel the *telos*, or directionality, of the entire process moving in and through your own nervous system, that is when you directly experience that movement as a vertical impulse in your own consciousness. You see that where we are headed is never static or predetermined. You awaken to what I sometimes call the "radical indeterminacy" of the life-process itself. As conditioned and mechanical as much of it might seem, the fact is that in every moment there is the possibility for novelty. In every moment there is the potential for something new. In every moment, there is room for emergence. That's the miracle of evolution.

WHEN EMERGENCE OCCURS IN MATTER or in biological life, it depends upon the *conditions* being just right. Cosmologists tell us, for example, that the moment when galaxies first formed, a billion years after the big bang, was the only moment that such an event could possibly have taken place. Before that moment, the universe was too dense, too hot, too close to the initial explosion. After that moment, it was too thin, too cool, too dispersed. Likewise, biologists tell us that for the evolutionary leap to take place in which single cells became a multi-celled organism, the conditions also had to be perfect.

What I have discovered is that the very same principle applies when we are trying to catalyze emergence at the level of consciousness and culture. The conditions must be right. In fact, I often use the metaphor of a "New Being" to describe this emergent cosmocentric cultural potential. Just as individual cells came together to make up a larger organism, autonomous, evolving individual human beings consciously come together to give rise to a dynamic greater *whole*. And this emergent potential of Evolutionary Enlightenment is completely dependent upon those individual cells—those autonomous, evolving beings—making the effort to understand and be a living expression of the inconceivably delicate balance of conditions that make it possible for it to come into existence.

Coming together beyond ego in the way I've been describing is much more than a spiritual exercise or even an ecstatic experience— it is a culturally creative act at the leading edge. The emergence of this enlightened we-space depends upon the right conditions being created and upheld by all the individuals involved. But creating perfect conditions is no small matter. When we are trying to catalyze emergence in our own individual and collective interior, the conditions we are talking about are not merely external circumstances but our own core values, our shared agreements, and our culturally constructed beliefs. No matter what new and thrilling potentials we may have glimpsed in a higher state of consciousness, unless our core cultural values shift in a significant way as a result of what we have seen, the future that we may have been inspired to create will never appear.

EVOLUTIONARY ENLIGHTENMENT IS ALWAYS about the evolution of culture itself through our own transformation. To the degree to which you are capable of embodying the evolutionary impulse, inevitably you will end up challenging the cultural ego within your own self. The cultural ego is the status quo, which lives in both our conscious and unconscious minds. It consists of all the deeply held images and conditioned beliefs that define for us what life is *supposed* to look like. It is impossible to separate any notion of individuality and personal identity from these core values that have such an influence on who we are and how we see the world.

The most challenging aspect of vertical spiritual development is the evolution of our value spheres. Given the right circumstances, it is not difficult to enter higher states of consciousness and in those higher states, to glimpse the exciting possibilities that await us on the other side of the status quo, beyond our predictable and fixed way of perceiving how things are. But it is another matter altogether to dislodge those predictable and rigid perspectives and embrace new and higher values.

Our shared values are not only pictures of what life *should* look like but also images of what's *possible*. In a spiritually enlightened, evolutionary worldview, our inner eye has awakened to the ever-forward-looking vision of the Authentic Self, with its limitless sense of possibility. Unless the limitations of our traditional, modern, and postmodern value spheres are brought into the light of awareness and penetrated with the eye of contemplation, it won't matter what thrilling new potentials we have glimpsed in higher states of consciousness; we won't be able to actualize them in real time. Unsupported by the ecstasy of those higher states, we will inevitably fall back into a limited self-structure and a value sphere that simply doesn't have space for the open-ended cosmic perspective of the Authentic Self.

I can't overemphasize how important this is. If we are passionately committed to the evolution of consciousness and culture, we must ensure at all costs that our conscious and unconscious shared values become an unambiguous expression of our deepest insights. Unless this is the case, the best part of each and every one of us—the spiritual impulse, our own Authentic Self—will inadvertently remain stunted in its ability to effect significant change in our world. It will stay imprisoned in unconscious preferences and unexamined values that bear no relationship whatsoever to our highest motives.

Eros, or the creative dimension of God, is that burning intelligence and driving impulse that is ever-leaning forward, reaching toward the emergence of that which has not yet become manifest. Evolutionary Enlightenment is about unapologetically becoming a living embodiment of those values that create the conditions for that unselfconscious creativity at the very edge of the possible.

THE ENTIRE NOTION OF EVOLUTIONARY BECOMING, or evolutionary emergence, is a new and unique orientation for the self. It's hard to even conceive of how different this orientation is from the ways we have traditionally and culturally been conditioned to relate to the human experience. With the exception of rare individuals throughout history, our orientation has generally been toward creating security, carving out a safe place in which to experience comfort and pleasure. Even revolutionaries who challenge the status quo in order to gain more rights and freedoms usually do so only until those rights and freedoms are achieved, after which they tend to settle in to a new status quo. Of course, there have always been rare individuals and inspired geniuses who are ever-reaching for that which is new, animated by the pulsation of the Authentic Self, who felt compelled to make significant progress and create new pathways in their particular fields. But what I'm speaking about here is not a particular type of genius or talent—it's a certain attitude and aspiration in relationship to the whole process of being alive. It's an attitude that the potential of this teaching is entirely dependent on, and that is completely contrary to the attitude that culture has conditioned us to have up to the present moment.

Inherent in human nature is the quest for certainty and the sense of security that is its reward. So there is always going to be a tension between the conditioned self's aspiration for security and the necessity to relinquish that aspiration in order to keep moving to higher stages without ever halting one's vertical development.

The shift in values that creates the conditions for perpetual emergence is a fundamental shift in orientation that is just beginning to dawn on us as we awaken to the fact that we are part of a process that is going somewhere. *Most human beings don't live for change.* Some of us live for achievement or greatness, but we don't live for perpetual change. I'm talking about disembedding ourselves from a deep, preconscious orientation toward stasis that has been created through thousands of years of history.

For the psychological ego and for the culturally conditioned self, living for change sounds unbearable. But for those of us who are awake to the evolutionary impulse, change becomes *home*. That feels more like home than any particular place in this world or any relationship with another human being. What feels like home is that sense of movement—vertical movement. In our emerging recognition of the evolutionary context that has given rise to our own presence here on Earth, we become more at home in perpetual movement than in comfort and stasis.

If you recognize the potential for emergence, in the inner dimensions of your own consciousness and our shared culture, then it is up to you to strive to create the perfect conditions in your life to support perpetual, vertically ascending change. The evolutionarily enlightened soul lives for change.

This is a fundamental shift. It is not just about freeing our minds from fixed ideas; it is about liberating ourselves from a static orientation to life. And it's not merely a personal shift; it is a very deep cultural change in the human psyche as a whole.

WHEN WE SPEAK ABOUT CREATING a new culture at the leading edge, beyond the status quo that we are embedded in, we don't necessarily know what it is supposed to look like. That's understandable—after all, it has not yet emerged. But we don't need to have a completely clear picture of where we are going. What we do need to know is what it means to disembed the self from that which is inhibiting its potential for vertical ascent. And as we free ourselves, in the midst of ascending, we *will* begin to see where it is that we are going. What is necessary, first and foremost, is to free the self to make this heroic journey.

The evolutionary process *is* going somewhere. Its next step is not predetermined, but now, maybe for the first time in history, we can participate with more conscious awareness than ever before in the *creation* of where it's going. When we make the effort to identify more with the vertical energy of the impulse to evolve than with the horizontal pull of the personal ego and culturally conditioned self, we transcend the enormous weight of our own traditional, modern, and postmodern value spheres. We open ourselves up to the liberating experience of that part of the cosmos that is trying to evolve through us in every moment. We make ourselves available to that powerful *telos* through shifting our attention and our shared values from the security of the conditioned past to the ever-ecstatic immediacy of the possible, *here and now*.

Unless we can make this shift, we will never be able to follow through on the promise of a teaching like this. The enormous promise of conscious evolution, of cultural emergence, will never be fulfilled beyond the experience of short-term inspiration unless this dynamic, primordial shift can be made at the core of yourself and in the inter-subjective we-space between a significant number of us. Otherwise, the internal gravity of the personal self and the cultural status quo will always inhibit our capacity for ongoing higher development.

Once it becomes clear what conditions are needed in order for emergence to take place, we must strive to create those conditions, no matter what it takes. If you engage with these teachings with great sincerity and urgency, your own consciousness and your relationships with others will become the stable structure through which new and higher expressions of meaning, purpose, and human potential can emerge in the evolving interior of the cosmos.

## CHAPTER 19

# Creating the Future

At the leading edge of our evolving consciousness and culture, where we awaken to the power of intersubjective nonduality, creativity flourishes. When we begin to share an enlightened cultural space in which the evolutionary impulse is emerging, we find ourselves experiencing a vertical momentum that is inherently creative. Indeed, the very source of God's cosmic surging forth, the wellspring of evolution's relentless reaching toward the future, becomes our shared location and self-sense.

This liberated space vibrates with a creative pulsation and is free from any sense of limitation. When you find yourself there, many new capacities and experiences emerge which, as far as I know, are not available or perceptible to us before we reach this cosmocentric stage. At the heart of this new order of human relatedness lies the ongoing interplay of several dynamic principles: the simultaneous experience of *autonomy* and *communion,* the vertical pull of *evolutionary tension*, and the generative spark of *creative friction.*

THE SIMULTANEOUS EMERGENCE of *autonomy* and *communion* is a rare and powerful experience. When the barriers between self and other fall away, we experience a higher *communion* beyond ego boundaries. But when this occurs among people who are awake to the evolutionary impulse, this communion is not just an undifferentiated harmony in which individuality and distinctions are erased. In fact, the very opposite is true. Paradoxically, at the very same time and in the very same space in which we are experiencing profound communion, the *autonomy* and creative potential of each individual emerges, free from self-consciousness. The simultaneous presence of liberated autonomy and ecstatic communion becomes the defining expression of one experience, one reality. This may be difficult to imagine, but when two or more people transcend ego together, such a seemingly paradoxical event *can* happen. And if human culture is to take an evolutionary leap forward, it *must* happen.

For real vertical movement to be sustained, communion alone is not enough. Out of the unity, *differentiation has to emerge.* Otherwise, even the experience of profound Oneness becomes developmentally inhibiting. Initially, that communion is such a new and ecstatic ground that all you want to do is remain there. But soon, it is no longer new territory, and in order for evolution to continue, unity has to give rise to differentiation. You have to step out of that unity as yourself, as an individuated force of the Authentic Self empowered by your own life experience, your unique talents and strengths. And when you do, you discover that your own uninhibited, autonomous, creative potential emerges without disturbing that context of ecstatic union.

Autonomy, in this context, means radical independence and spiritual authenticity. It emerges when you are standing alone, in a state of self-reliance and passionate interest in the evolutionary process. Autonomy is the expression of creative freedom—the powerful, unrestricted ability to flower in your own potential without limit. When you discover true autonomy, you awaken to a fullness of self that is dramatically free from self-consciousness. You simply are who you are, ecstatically experiencing your own authenticity spontaneously manifesting itself. Communion, in this context, is the profound revelation of intersubjective nonduality that I've been describing. It is the liberating experience of the Authentic Self recognizing itself in others—the many coming together as One in egoless freedom and the mutual conscious intention to evolve.

For both autonomy and communion to exist simultaneously is a paradox—two apparently conflicting capacities are able to coexist. This can only happen in a context of intersubjective enlightened awareness. In enlightened awareness, paradoxes are mysteriously resolved. Usually, there is a conflict between autonomy and communion. When an individual experiences powerful autonomy, it's often at the expense of communion with others. To realize our creative freedom, we may feel the need to withdraw from relatedness so we are free to flower and flourish. And to experience communion, we find that we almost always have to sacrifice some degree of our autonomy in order to harmoniously come together with others. In Evolutionary Enlightenment, however, a dynamic field is created where the one and the many are literally the same and yet remain differentiated. It is a new and evolving expression of nonduality in which self and other seamlessly merge, and yet miraculously do not become indistinct. And then consciousness delights in pursuing its own creative potential in ecstatic collaboration with itself.

THIS LIBERATED CREATIVITY IS FELT in the human heart and mind as a powerful wakefulness, a thoroughly positive and wholesome *evolutionary tension*, that compels you to rise to your highest potential. Often we relate to tension as being negative, but *evolutionary* tension is inherently positive. It is that very same forward-reaching energy in consciousness that you feel when you become aware of a mysterious sense of purpose and responsibility for something higher than the concerns of your own ego. It's a heightened intensity that awakens your soul, and compels you to sit up straight, focus, and pay attention. Evolutionary tension is an upward pull, a profound sense of urgency to bring into manifestation that which has not yet occurred. It is the relentless demand to *become more,* to reach for new and ever-higher levels of moral, philosophical, and spiritual maturity. This positive tension creates a potent and spiritually charged context for human relationship because it is infused with the living presence of the possible.

Evolutionary tension is the experiential quality of the new consciousness that is liberated between individuals who come together in autonomy and communion. Intersubjective nonduality is more than just the experience of peace and bliss. In fact, when you come together with others who are committed to the evolution of consciousness and culture, you are choosing to associate with a spiritual intensity and demand that is going to be excruciating for your ego. That's what authentic, evolutionarily enlightened spiritual partnership is all about. It is a kind of relatedness that would be almost unbearable if one wasn't living for perpetual change. But for your Authentic Self, that tension is experienced as ecstasy, and it wants nothing more than to live every moment at the heart of that spiritual intensity. It thrives on the *creative friction* that is generated in the crucible of evolutionary becoming.

CREATIVE FRICTION IS THE VERY ENGINE of conscious evolution at the leading edge. The presence of ongoing creative friction in a context of autonomy and communion is what indicates deep spiritual, psychological, and emotional health and vibrancy in this type of intersubjective, or collective, context. In fact, I am convinced that authentic spiritual friendship—where human beings are evolutionary partners, lovers of life, God, and Spirit—requires individuals to come together and *conflict* with each other in the most creative way possible. Consciously engaging with each other and the life-process, we strive to deconstruct and transcend old structures and creatively construct new and more relevant ones. Creative friction is the very spiritual lifeblood of the new culture that we need to create.

Often, those of us who are interested in higher consciousness tend to be attached to the perennial spiritual ideals of peace, harmony, love, and bliss. We don't generally associate notions like friction, tension, or conflict with spirituality. But if you are interested in spiritual *evolution,* you will find that these qualities can be powerful expressions of Spirit in action. Indeed, without evolutionary tension and creative friction, higher development cannot and will not occur.

This is true at every level of the creative process. Was the big bang a peaceful event? When stars collided so that new elements could be born, was that a harmonious occasion? The ongoing process of material evolution has unfolded through extraordinary force and violence. And in the domain of biological evolution, the same truth holds. Nature is ruthless and brutal—"red in tooth and claw," as the saying goes. Our own bodies depend on conflict—the immune system is designed to fight and destroy to ensure our physical survival. Even the process that creates new life—the sexual encounter—is a kind of friction.

If we look at the evolution of culture, the same principle holds true: development requires friction. For evolution to occur, the creative process demands that we transcend the old in order to give rise to the new. And this kind of transition inevitably will create conflict—friction between the status quo and the higher values, bigger perspectives, and new potentials that are trying to emerge. When you begin to see the whole process from a cosmocentric vantage point, you will understand that conflict and creative friction is simply an inherent and essential part of the developmental unfolding.

Did you know that human beings only develop through interaction with each other? If you take a little baby out of human society and leave her to grow up among wolves, she is not going to develop in the ways other children do—her psychological structures are not going to evolve beyond the most primitive levels. Adult development works in the same way. For all but the rarest exceptions, the evolution of our own consciousness is largely dependent upon how profound our engagement is with the culture around us. So in an evolved spiritual context, the nature and purpose of human relationship would be a creative friction at the highest level that would mutually ensure ongoing individual and collective development. This may come as a surprise to some, but when life is only peaceful and calm, there is little fertile ground for evolution.

It's not difficult to see this at the physical level. For example, if you only eat and sleep, what's going to happen to your body? Will it develop? Of course not. But if you add evolutionary tension and creative friction by exercising your muscles and your skeletal structure, something positive and developmental begins to occur. The same thing happens with your intellect. If you just read comic books and watch television, and don't make the effort to exercise your cognitive and conceptual capacities, what happens? Your mind doesn't develop. But when you're applying evolutionary tension and creative friction on an intellectual level—through challenging yourself to think in more complex ways, and to dialogue and debate with others—your capacity for intellectual depth, abstract thinking, and subtle discrimination will grow and develop.

At the highest level, the level of consciousness, this same principle applies. And it is within the awakened field of intersubjective nonduality—the space between subjects who have awakened to Eros—that creative friction and evolutionary tension can drive a profound process of cultural development in the interior of the cosmos.

Remember, the relationships we engage in and the values we share create the structures of the intersubjective dimension, which *is* culture. If you are truly dedicated to creating a more evolved world, the future is not some far-off fantasy realm but is something you forge in and through your relationships with other people right now. The intersubjective we-space between such inspired individuals becomes a creative vortex in which something is being born every moment out of the spiritual, moral, intellectual, and philosophical friction. Together, you become a portal through which evolution occurs.

ONCE AGAIN, THE RECOGNITION that evolutionary tension and creative friction drives both the internal and external development of the cosmos can challenge some of our most fundamental spiritual ideals and assumptions. For example, if you believe that Spirit or God equals peace and love, it makes sense that you would see all forms of conflict, tension, and friction as inherently negative, as well as antithetical to higher human development. And many of them certainly are. But in an evolutionary worldview, we are compelled to redefine who and what God actually is, and what love really means.

In the unmanifest dimension, the ground of Being—that perfect, empty no-place where there is only absolute stillness—you *could* say that God is peace. Before the universe was born, resting in that state of perfection and ease, it could not have been more peaceful, because nothing had yet occurred. But when God decided to *become,* to take form, this whole process of creation and destruction, friction and emergence, was set in motion. That is what you are, that is what I am, and that is also the nature of God, in the manifest realm.

What does this new understanding of God have to do with love? This is an important question, because the common idea is that love is God, and God is love. And to many of us, spiritual love means compassion, forgiveness, and unconditional acceptance. That *is* one kind of love. But that kind of love is the expression of God as *Being*—the reflection of the mystical revelation that everything is already perfect. What happens to love when God becomes the evolutionary impulse, or Eros? That's the emergence of a very different form of love—the expression of God as *Becoming*. In an evolutionary worldview, God's purpose is perpetual development, or vertical ascent. So in this context, the expression of the greatest love is an *insistence* on higher development. It is not the kind of love that's going to accept you as you are. It's a kind of love that always wants more, and is therefore always challenging to the status quo of the personal ego and the culturally conditioned self. No matter how far you have come, there will always be farther to go. This love is infused with evolutionary tension, and it generates creative friction.

The idea of God as peace and Love as compassion is an ancient ideal, one that took root in the human heart and mind long before the knowledge of evolution emerged. While it remains as powerful and as relevant ever, this idea of God is only half of the picture. Now we understand the nature of God to be both Being and Becoming, emptiness and Eros. And discovering what God as Eros actually looks like and feels like within us and between us is new territory. When you embrace this evolutionary interpretation of who and what God is, then you realize that yes, God *is* love but love is a dynamic and dramatic *will* toward higher emergence. It is God trying to evolve, through you and through me, and most importantly, through *us*.

# CHAPTER 20

# The Edge of Evolution

A HUMAN BEING TRYING TO CATALYZE THE EMERGENCE of a higher level of consciousness is like a rocket ship trying to break free from the Earth's gravity. The gravity that we are endeavoring to release ourselves from is the historical weight of our conditioning, both personal and cultural. If we can generate enough vertical momentum to propel us beyond the boundaries of who we have been, even if only temporarily, we will find ourselves in uncharted territory. But if we want to not only visit that new terrain but become permanent residents, to create a new culture there together, the task confronting us is even greater. Once we have broken through that gravity for long enough to experience the freedom of space, we must create the stable structures that will allow us to remain there.

Endeavoring to stabilize a newly emergent cultural worldspace in this way is like breaking through the atmosphere and then attempting to build a space station—a huge structure suspended outside of the normal field of gravity. And when the space we are moving into is the outer reaches of our subjective and intersubjective consciousness, the structure we are striving to build is made up of new shared cultural agreements about the meaning and purpose of life. To give rise to the next stage beyond postmodernity, these agreements need to be based upon a deep-time evolutionary worldview, a developmental understanding of human history, and an appreciation of the fact that as the self evolves, culture evolves.

This intersubjective construction project has barely begun. Imagine a space station that is only in the first stages of being built. The skeleton of its structure is there, but it's very unstable, because large parts of it are not yet in place. You can get a sense of what it will look like, but it is still so incomplete that if even one piece were to fall away, the entire construct would break apart. That's what the process of building intersubjective cultural structures is like, particularly in the beginning. The pieces are human beings—men and women just like you and me who have layer upon layer of conditioned habits and tendencies that do not necessarily support a higher emergence. Inevitably, we will find that we are trying to create a new culture while we remain deeply embedded in the old one. At the leading edge, we are actually trying to pioneer an authentic transition to post-postmodern cultural agreements and to stabilize them. And because our center of gravity tends to lie more in the old than it does in the new, this new structure will be very fragile.

Entering into unexplored territory, and staying there, is an enormous challenge. But if we can take these bold steps forward, heroically embracing higher ideals and bigger perspectives like those described here, then slowly but surely, the new structures will stabilize. In the end, it's only our spiritual inspiration and commitment to evolutionary emergence that will hold the pieces in place, even while the larger structure remains unstable. It's our individual willingness to hold steady, no matter what, for the sake of the evolution of consciousness and culture, as ourselves. If we can do this, then the stability of our spiritual attainment and the depth of our relationships with each other will become the underlying framework upon which cultural evolution can establish itself at new heights.

IF YOU ARE TRYING TO do something genuinely new, you have to be a pioneer, you have to be a change-agent. In order to contribute to creating the future, you need to be aligned with the very edge of evolution. Otherwise, you are going to be following the beaten path, living out the patterns that have been formed by countless others. Most human beings are born and die within a preexistent cultural context that we don't necessarily feel is up to us to define. Without even knowing it, we tend to do what everyone else is doing. But at this particular time in history, for these new evolutionary stages, structures, and potentials to emerge, it requires rare and heroic men and women who have awakened to the conviction that this next step needs to happen and that we're the ones who have to take it.

How many of us are willing to bear the emotional, psychological, philosophical, and spiritual overwhelm of being real pioneers? It's all too easy to sit back, observe the evolutionary challenges confronting our world, and fall into a state of despair or cynicism. It takes courage to be a change-agent. And it takes spiritual self-confidence. Spiritual self-confidence is a confidence in your own Authentic Self—in the driving impulse behind this creative process that we are all part of. If you live the five tenets of Evolutionary Enlightenment as if your life depended on it, you will align yourself with that deeper dimension of who you are, and you *will* develop spiritual self-confidence.

Spiritual confidence is the heaviest anchor in the midst of the unending storm that is life and death. It is an unshakable confidence in the inherent positivity of the life-process itself—in the rightness of finding oneself at the very edge of the evolving cosmos, in all its chaos and complexity. Having this kind of confidence is of the utmost importance for anyone who cares deeply about the way things are— and even more so for the courageous change-agent who wants to create something new, who would dare to be the one to stand for and bear witness to that which is higher.

Being an evolutionary change-agent means living on the very edge of this vast process, knowing that it has taken fourteen billion years to reach this point, and actively endeavoring to move the entire process forward through your own transformation. It won't be easy, but I have no doubt that for those of us who have glimpsed the glory of our higher potentials, this is what we are here to do.

I don't believe that the clarity and liberation of mystical insight is a free ride. I am convinced that the awakening of the spiritual impulse in our own hearts and minds is actually an evolutionary trigger—an urgent whisper from the Self to Itself, God's quiet voice imploring us to relinquish our attachment to our culturally conditioned relativism, our materialism, and our narcissism. Why are we being called? So we will take responsibility for the evolution of our own consciousness and culture, in such a way that raises the bar for all of us at the leading edge.

When we're talking about pushing that edge, there's always going to be an element of enormous risk. Evolution is a messy process. There are no guarantees. So anybody who really wants to strive for something new is going to have to be willing to make mistakes, take wrong turns, and even to fail. The simple truth is this: If not failing is more important to you than genuinely succeeding, you're never going to make it. If you want to succeed, you must have the spiritual self-confidence, heroic will, tenacity, courage, and commitment to fearlessly engage with the evolutionary process until something profound, mysterious, and extraordinary happens that cannot be undone.

WHEN YOU ARE LIVING THIS FULLY and fearlessly in the evolutionary passion and perspective of the Authentic Self, then something extraordinary *does* begin to happen. The unmanifest potential of the near future flickers into awareness and even in brief moments seems to actually become manifest in the present moment. And when we meet others in this same heightened state of consciousness, together we can see and feel, directly cognize, and intuit a compelling future that is possible to create here and now, in the present moment—not as a remote ideal but as the most screamingly imminent potential imaginable. Finding each other—finding those other individuals who feel as passionately as we do about the evolution of consciousness and culture—liberates and uplifts our spirits and gives us the inspiration to take bold steps we otherwise might not have the courage to take.

When many individuals experience simultaneously the promise of the next moment, it means the evolutionary impulse is calling us to give rise to its next step. Indeed, we are compelled to be the future that we can see—the future that is emerging in the field of our awareness so clearly that it seems we are already there. But the promise of such moments poses a greater challenge than may first be apparent. Because you can see them so clearly, it is easy to assume that the higher levels of consciousness you are experiencing already exist, and all you need to do is step into them. But in fact, most often, what you are seeing is only a potential, not an actual preexisting level that simply needs to be reached.

This is very important to understand. The future is not a given. What's going to happen is not already known and is not predetermined. The higher stages of consciousness and culture that lie in front of us *do not yet exist.* This sounds like a simple point, but it is profound. Many of us who are spiritually inspired tend to subscribe to metaphysical worldviews that tell us that the higher levels and stages of development are already laid out. But they're not. The newly emerging potentials in consciousness and culture have not yet appeared with enough consistency to become self-existing levels, or new "habits" in the interior fabric of the cosmos. They only come into being to the degree that you and I consciously participate together to develop those higher capacities in ourselves.

It is always those individuals who are ahead of their time, living on the leading edge, who participate in the creation of these new structures or habits in consciousness. Eventually, when others progress through the already established stages of cultural development, they're going to follow in the footsteps of those evolutionary pioneers who went before them. When enough people take the new path, it will become, over time, an established cultural stage. But at this moment in our shared history, the next stage has barely been laid down. This is why the awakening human at the leading edge today bears such a profound responsibility to be an evolutionary pioneer—to be the one who is literally living in that place between the present and the future.

Living in that place means that the next stage of development exists in your own awareness as an ever-present but as-yet-unmanifest potential, right now. With this emerging intuition of the future, your consciousness expands and you have the experience of being intensely awake. Why? Because your conscious, living relationship with the future enlightens your relationship to the present moment, fills it with conscience, purpose, and direction. And then your active, participatory relationship with life today becomes an expression of your creative responsibility to give rise to the new world of tomorrow.

WHAT THAT ACTUALLY MEANS IS AN ever-new revelation for me—that, as audacious as it may sound, the depth of our conscious engagement with the life-process right now is potentially the creative edge of evolution itself. And an evolutionary worldview reveals to us that there is neither a predetermined blueprint for where we are going nor a foreseeable end to the process. Of course, if you are aspiring for spiritual freedom and are awake to the limitless potential of the evolutionary impulse, then nothing is going to be more exciting than living on that edge yourself.

This is what's so thrilling about an evolutionary approach to spiritual enlightenment—the profound implications of the recognition that contrary to the beliefs of the great traditions and the popular convictions of New Age thinking, *nothing is predestined*. The future is *not* already known. And God, when understood to be the energy and intelligence that initiated the creative process, is not separate from the entire event. That's the whole point: from an awakened perspective, the evolutionary process is not dualistic. Whoever or whatever created the process is not separate from or outside the process itself.

Indeed, life gets a lot more interesting when you come to terms with the fact that that creative impulse, that cosmic energy and intelligence, is not outside the process and ultimately is not separate from your own consciousness, from your own capacity to cognize the entire unfolding here and now. That's when you awaken to a new level of spiritual maturity: when you realize that God does not necessarily know any more about where we are all going than you do in your best moments.

For those of us at the leading edge at this critical moment in human history, what could make the meaning and purpose of spiritual enlightenment more apparent? What could make more sense or be more compelling on an emotional, intellectual, philosophical, and spiritual level than the simple recognition that *"It is up to me"?* God is evolving as we evolve. And this moment itself, assuming that you are leaning into it with all of your being, reaching for the future, is potentially the very edge of the possible.

## ABOUT THE AUTHOR

Andrew Cohen is a spiritual teacher, cultural visionary, and founder of the global nonprofit EnlightenNext and its award-winning publication *EnlightenNext* magazine. Since 1986, Cohen has been traveling the world giving public lectures and leading intensive retreats. Through his writings, teachings, and ongoing dialogues with leading philosophers, scientists, and mystics, he has become known as one of the defining voices of the new evolutionary spirituality.

Born in New York City in 1955 and raised in a secular Jewish family, Cohen had his passion for spirit unexpectedly ignited at the age of sixteen, when a spontaneous revelation of "cosmic consciousness" opened his eyes to a new dimension of life. Some years later, as a result of that experience, he gave up aspirations to become a musician and dedicated himself wholeheartedly to its rediscovery. After several years of intensive spiritual pursuit in the United States, including the study of martial arts, Kriya Yoga, and Buddhist meditation, Cohen followed the footsteps of a generation of Western seekers to India. It was there, in the land of the sages, that he met his last teacher H.W.L. Poonja, a disciple of the revered Ramana Maharshi, in 1986. In just a few short weeks, Cohen experienced a life-changing awakening, the story of which was told in his first book, *My Master Is My Self*. Shortly afterwards, with his teacher's blessing, Cohen began to teach.

Always an independent thinker, Cohen soon diverged from the traditional Eastern approach that had catalyzed his own awakening, with its emphasis on transcendence and the illusory nature of the phenomenal world. Grappling with questions and challenges that arose as he sought to bring the revelation of enlightenment to a contemporary Western audience, he gradually forged his own original spiritual teaching, Evolutionary Enlightenment. A modern-day equivalent of the ancient wisdom teachings, Cohen's work is no footnote to tradition but a distinct and innovative synthesis. He has brought the timeless depth of enlightened wisdom into the twenty-first century and significantly redirected its purpose and promise—calling not for transcendence of worldly attachment, or even for compassionate care and service, but for a deep and heroic responsibility for the *evolution* of the world. In this, he finds more in common with the great evolutionary visionaries of the last century, such as Sri Aurobindo and Pierre Teilhard de Chardin, than he does with the ancient Eastern enlightenment tradition in which his own awakening occurred. To both these streams of thought he adds a further element: a rich and nuanced understanding of the practical dynamics of individual and cultural transformation at our particular moment in history.

Cohen's interest in cultural evolution is much more than theoretical. For more than two decades he has been intensively engaged with committed individuals and groups from around the world who are striving to put his teachings into practice. This engagement has, in turn, informed his thinking, creating a dynamic and fertile interplay between vision and practice, ideal and reality. Among the many fruits of this work, perhaps the most significant has been a series of breakthroughs into collective or *intersubjective* higher states of consciousness, and the active translation of these insights into new values, perspectives, and principles that are enabling individuals to lay the foundations for a new cultural paradigm. The results of this living inquiry are embraced and shared by a growing global movement of "Evolutionaries."

In addition to his work as a teacher, Cohen is also dedicated to changing the cultural conversation about the purpose and significance of spiritual enlightenment in our time. This is best seen in the magazine he founded in 1991, *EnlightenNext* (formerly *What Is Enlightenment?*), which has become the premier forum for serious discussion at the intersection of spirituality and culture. In its pages, and the live forums that have grown out of them, Cohen and his team of collaborators have engaged spiritual, religious, cultural, and scientific thought leaders in a dynamic inquiry about the nature of inner and outer evolution. Cohen's unusual perspective and commitment to dialogue have led to invitations to speak at numerous forums over the years, including the Parliament of the World's Religions (2004, 2009), LOHAS International Conference, International Transpersonal Conference, Integral Leadership in Action, and the International Conference on the Frontiers of Yoga and Consciousness Research, as well as universities, spiritual centers, and business settings around the world.

EnlightenNext has centers worldwide, and members in more than twenty countries. Cohen lives at the organization's world headquarters in Lenox, Massachusetts, and spends several months of the year traveling, teaching, and leading retreats around the world.

For more information about Andrew Cohen's work and his upcoming teachings and retreats, visit www.andrewcohen.org.

## BOOKS BY ANDREW COHEN

*My Master Is My Self*

*Enlightenment Is a Secret*

*An Unconditional Relationship to Life*

*Freedom Has No History*

*Embracing Heaven & Earth*

*Living Enlightenment*